The Virgin of the World

Ancient Mysteries of Creation, Divinity, and the Soul

A Modern Translation

Adapted for the Contemporary Reader

Hermes Trismegistus

Table of Contents

Preface - Message to the Reader

Rebuilding the Greatest Library in Human History

Thousands of years ago, the Library of Alexandria was the heart of global knowledge — a sanctuary where the wisdom of every known civilization was gathered and shared freely.

And then, it was lost.

Now, we're rebuilding it — and you are invited to join us.

At the Library of Alexandria, we've set out to make every book available to *every person on Earth* — not just in print, but in every language, every format, and for every reader.

Here's how we do it:

- **Deluxe Print Editions at True Printing Cost** - Order any book as a high-quality paperback, elegant hardcover, or stunning boxset — and only pay what it costs to print. No markups. No middlemen.

- **Unlimited Access to the Greatest Works** - Enjoy thousands of timeless classics — from Plato to Shakespeare to Tolstoy — in beautiful, modern eBook and audiobook editions. Read and listen without limits — for every reader, everywhere.

- **Modern Translations for Every Language & Dialect** - We're reimagining the classics in clear, accessible language — and translating them into every dialect imaginable. Everyone deserves to understand humanity's greatest ideas.

When you visit **LibraryofAlexandria.com**, you're not just accessing books — you're joining a global movement to restore, preserve, and share the wisdom of civilization.

Join us today at LibraryofAlexandria.com

Together, we'll ensure the light of human wisdom never fades again.

With gratitude,
The Modern Library of Alexandria Team

Visit:

www.libraryofalexandria.com

Or scan the code below:

Introduction

THE HERMETIC BOOKS

These books were very well-known and later became highly valued by those seeking to use them for alchemical purposes, especially for making gold. The Roman Emperor Severus gathered all writings about the Mysteries and buried them in the tomb of Alexander the Great. Diocletian destroyed their alchemy books to prevent Egypt from becoming so wealthy that it could no longer be a dependent state. These writings, containing the laws, science, and theology of Egypt, were said by priests to have been written during the time of the gods, before the reign of the first human king, Menes. Ancient monuments contain references that confirm how old these writings are. There were four main books, which were divided into forty-two volumes altogether. These numbers are the same as the Vedas, which, according to the Puranas, were brought to Egypt by the Yadavas during the first migration from India. The subjects in these books were also similar, though it's still unclear to what extent the Books of Hermes were copied from the Vedas.

These books were kept in the innermost parts of the temples, and only the highest-ranking priests were allowed to read them. They were treated with great respect and carried during important religious ceremonies. The chief priests were responsible for ten volumes that discussed the creation of the world, the gods' nature, and divine laws for priests. Prophets carried four volumes that dealt with astronomy and astrology. The leader of the sacred musicians held two volumes with hymns to the gods and advice on how the king should behave, which the singer had to memorize. These hymns were considered so ancient and sacred that Plato said they were attributed to Isis and believed to be ten thousand years old. Temple workers carried ten more volumes, which contained prayers, rules for offerings, and instructions for festivals and processions. The remaining volumes focused on philosophy and sciences, including anatomy and medicine.

The Books of Hermes, once renowned, have been lost for about fifteen hundred years. The fragments found in this collection have been carefully studied. In the early days of Christianity, these writings were held in high regard and considered genuine. Christian scholars often referred to them to support Christian beliefs, and the writer Lactantius, known as the "Christian Cicero," said, "Hermes, I don't know how, has discovered nearly the whole truth." Hermes was seen as a divine messenger, and his writings were thought to represent the ancient Egyptian religion in which Moses was trained. This view was supported by Renaissance scholars like Marsilio Ficino and Patricius, who believed these works influenced Orphic rituals and the philosophies of Pythagoras and Plato.

However, doubts about the authenticity of these writings arose. Some scholars thought they were written by a Jew, others by a Christian or a Gnostic, based on the content. Modern critics, including Dr. Louis Menard, now believe these writings are among the latest works of Greek philosophy. But within these texts, which reflect Alexandrian ideas, traces of ancient Egyptian religious thought still remain. Menard suggests that the Egyptian philosophy recorded in the Books of Hermes was the result of blending Egyptian religious ideas with Greek philosophical concepts. These books are the only surviving record of that Egyptian philosophy, presenting old beliefs and ideas in abstract terms instead of their original mythological form.

The arrival of Christianity may seem at first like a sudden and complete change in the beliefs and practices of the Western world. However, history shows that such transformations don't happen overnight. To understand how one religion replaces another, it's important not to focus only on their most extreme differences— like comparing Homer's mythology with the Christian symbols from the Council of Nicaea. Instead, it's essential to explore the gradual shifts and connections between them over time.

It is important to study the remaining works from this period of transition, when ancient Greek ideas were being reshaped through discussions and mixed with religions from the East that were spreading into Europe. Christianity is the latest example of how these Eastern beliefs influenced the West. It didn't arrive suddenly, shocking the old world. Instead, it took time to develop, with its ideas forming alongside those in Greece, Asia, and Egypt.

Many of the same problems that Christianity aimed to solve were already being discussed in these regions. The ideas in the air at that time blended in different ways.

The rise of many different religious sects today only gives a small sense of how dynamic the intellectual activity was back then. Alexandria was at the heart of this development, acting as a center for moral and philosophical exploration. People were debating big questions like the nature of evil, the purpose of souls, their downfall, and their redemption. The ultimate prize for answering these questions was control over people's beliefs, and in the end, Christianity offered the solution that prevailed.

Our critic looks at the books of Hermes Trismegistus and tries to figure out what parts reflect Egyptian thought and what might have come from Jewish ideas. He points out that when we encounter ideas that resemble those of Plato or Pythagoras, we need to ask if the author rediscovered the same ancient sources that Plato and Pythagoras had used or if these ideas represent something purely Greek. This raises questions about how much Eastern thought influenced Greek philosophy. People tend to overestimate the impact of Eastern ideas on Greek thought, partly because the Greeks themselves believed in that influence. However, the real exchange between Greek and other cultures only became steady and meaningful after Alexandria was founded. During these exchanges, Greece had more to share with other cultures than it received from them. The people of the East, including those who interacted with the Greeks, didn't have what we would call a formal philosophy. They lacked traditions of analyzing the mind, searching for the foundations of knowledge and moral rules, and applying these ideas to society. These concepts were new to the East before Alexander the Great's conquests.

Plato mentions a comment from an Egyptian priest who told the Greeks, "You are just children; there are no elders among you." This could reflect the attitude of Egypt and other Eastern cultures. The spirit of scientific inquiry and political instinct was unfamiliar to these peoples. While they could endure for long periods, they never seemed to mature. They were like grown children, still being guided by others and unable to pursue truth or achieve justice on their own.

The East, having learned philosophy from Greece, could only offer what it had—deep religious feelings. Greece, tired of the skepticism caused by disagreements among its philosophical schools, welcomed this religious intensity. This shift toward spiritual enthusiasm was a sign of the need for renewed faith. The books of Hermes Trismegistus serve as a bridge between past beliefs and future ones, linking ideas from the old world to the new. Though these writings are part of pagan thought, they reflect the final moments of paganism. Paganism resisted the new faith and refused to surrender to it, guarding the knowledge of the old civilization that was fading. It accepted its fate, ready to rest forever in its birthplace—ancient Egypt, the land of the dead.

Dr. Menard concludes that the Hermetic books are the last remains of paganism. They belong to both Greek philosophy and Egyptian religion, and their mystical nature connects them to the Middle Ages. These writings lie between two eras—one ending and the other beginning—like creatures that bridge different species but are not fully part of either group. As a result, they are not as great as the religious beliefs of Homer's time or Christianity, but they help us understand the transition from one to the other. They contain both emerging beliefs and those fading away, meeting and intertwining as one era gives way to the next.

To challenge and correct the earlier statements about the relationship between Greek and Eastern thought, we offer the following insights from Mr. Plumptre's "History of Pantheism." From childhood, most of us are taught to believe that we owe all our knowledge of theology and religion to the Hebrews, and much of our understanding of God as well. At the same time, we are told that the Greeks gave us all our knowledge of the arts, sciences, philosophy, and wisdom. Similarly, we are taught to credit the Romans for shaping our ideas about discipline and law. While these definitions are generally accurate for our connections with the Hebrews and Romans, the same cannot be said about the Greeks.

The statement is somewhat accurate. It is true that we owe much of our knowledge to the Greeks. However, the error lies in assuming that the Greeks were the first to pursue learning purely for its own sake, that they received no knowledge from other cultures, and that they invented it all themselves. This view might also suggest that they were the first people to reach a high level of civilization. Even a basic understanding of Egyptian or Hindu history is enough to show how mistaken this idea is. Egyptian civilization stretches so far back in history that it is almost impossible to pinpoint its beginning. It is now widely accepted that Moses gained much of his knowledge from the Egyptians, meaning that even our earliest religious ideas may have come from Egypt.

Mr. Plumptre points out that while both the Hindus and Egyptians had developed advanced religious and philosophical systems long ago, the Greeks remained trapped in ignorance and superstition. This changed dramatically after a key event that sparked Greek intellectual development and transformed Greece from a state of childish ignorance into a leading cultural and philosophical power. That event was the opening of Egypt's ports by King Psammetichus in 670 B.C. Until that time, Egypt had been closed off from Europe and the Mediterranean with restrictions as strict as those once seen in China and Japan. To the Greeks, Egypt was nothing more than a land of mystery and myth, as reflected in the works of Homer and Hesiod. When Egypt finally opened up, the effect on Europe's development was profound and far-reaching. Greece, followed by the rest of the world, owed its civilization to this event. It shattered belief in old myths and gave birth to Greek philosophy.

This statement needs some adjustment, though. While Greek myths might seem like irrational stories without deeper meaning, they were actually symbols hiding important spiritual truths. Their early presence in Greece shows that institutions dedicated to sacred mysteries existed long before Greek philosophy emerged. The fact that these mysteries shared ideas with Egypt and the East also reveals that there was religious contact between these regions long before trade, political connections, or philosophical exchanges took place. Christian missionary work was not the first of its kind; the sacred mysteries were constantly spreading, establishing themselves in new places even ahead of secular civilizations. The migration of Abraham, the travels of Bacchus, and the journey of Moses are all examples of this kind of movement.

Mr. Plumptre concludes that any similarities between Greek and Egyptian philosophy were the result of the Greeks adopting ideas from Egypt. It seems impossible to disagree with this conclusion. We believe that Menard's differing opinion comes from his focus on classical knowledge without considering Hermetic and Kabbalistic traditions. Since these traditions contain the spiritual history of the world, ignoring them makes it impossible to fully understand these topics. Those who rely only on conventional methods of learning and reject anything beyond surface-level knowledge tend to dismiss the idea that a hidden, divine system of teachings has existed since ancient times. Yet, this conclusion is unavoidable based on the overwhelming evidence, both from public sources and secret teachings.

The earliest traces of this knowledge can be found in India and Egypt. If there are similarities between the ancient teachings of these lands and those of Greece, Judea, and Christianity, it is because the same truths were passed from one culture to another. These truths were reshaped to fit the needs and spirit of each time and place. This process will continue until humanity either falls into complete ignorance and no longer cares about truth or reaches a state of enlightenment where truth is fully understood and preserved as our most valuable treasure forever.

Regardless of the debate, even the most critical arguments must admit three key points. First, some of the teachings in the Hermetic texts are truly ancient, originating from Egypt, making them authentically Hermetic. Second, there are clear similarities between these ancient Hermetic teachings and the ideas found in Christianity. And third, the Church has acknowledged and accepted these similarities, showing that Christianity, rather than being a completely new and original belief system when it first began, is actually a continuation or reworking of ideas that had existed long before.

THE HERMETIC SYSTEM AND THE SIGNIFICANCE OF ITS PRESENT REVIVAL

For anyone studying humanity, one of the most important features of our current era is the revival of occult science and mystical, or hidden, philosophy. This revival is important not just because of the ideas themselves, but also because of the timing. It is happening during a period when the human mind, as represented by modern thinkers, seemed to have fully embraced materialism. However, this shift toward materialism turned out to be temporary, as some people—those attuned to the deeper connections of life and aware of the unity within nature—already knew. Just as the sun's return begins at its lowest point, spiritual renewal follows times of decline. When materialism threatened to extinguish the spiritual awareness of humanity, the return of mystical and occult teachings brought that awareness back to life.

History has shown that the end of old religious forms often signals the beginning of new and better spiritual insights. Those who believe in the divine nature of the human spirit trusted that, in time, it would rise up against materialism. They see the current revival as that very awakening. This revival is also noteworthy because it has brought Hermetic philosophy back into the spotlight for the first time in centuries. Every major religious awakening in history has involved this philosophy in some way. Hermetic Gnosis— an ancient system with roots going back to prehistoric Egypt—

has been the foundation of many religious and philosophical traditions across the East and the West. Both Buddhism and Christianity were intended to express its teachings, although this was only recognized by a select few. Even the mystical school that flourished during the Middle Ages, which brought great prestige to the church, was secretly based on the same ideas.

That school aimed to rescue religion from being reduced to rituals, historical events, and the control of a materialistic clergy. Instead, it sought to restore religion's true spiritual and intuitive nature. Although this effort did not achieve lasting success, it was not because of any flaw in the system. The challenge lay in the fact that the spiritual awareness required to fully understand the teachings was something only a few people possessed at that time. The world simply was not ready for a philosophy that represented reason at its highest level. Now, however, it is clear that the revival we are witnessing is just one in a series of similar movements throughout history. Given the current changes in society, there is good reason to believe this revival will succeed more than any before it.

Even though the state of society today may seem bleak in many areas—whether in social issues, philosophy, morality, or religion—there has never been a time when conditions were better for a major positive change. New ideas and knowledge now spread faster than ever, and the hardships and dissatisfaction people are experiencing have made them more open to change. As a result, Hermetic philosophy now has a better chance of gaining acceptance than ever before. In the past, it was embraced by the brightest minds and most honorable individuals. With the right presentation, it is likely that this philosophy will find a place in the hearts and minds of people in this new era.

There are already signs that the church, still a powerful force, may support this revival—not only to preserve itself but also to protect religious truth. The importance of Pope Leo XIII's decision to restore the works of Aquinas as the foundation for church education is not yet widely understood. However, for those initiated in the teachings of Hermes, this move is seen as a reason for great optimism. A similar view applies to the strange, though sometimes misguided, phenomenon of modern spiritualism.

With these thoughts on the circumstances surrounding the revival—of which this collection of writings is both a product and a tool—we will now provide a brief overview of the nature of the teachings that have played such a major role in the past and seem likely to have even greater impact in the future.

It's important to mention that this overview isn't limited to the Hermetic fragments found in these reprints. These fragments are incomplete, and some parts have been altered or corrupted over time, though they still contain profound and valuable teachings. Much of what remains is written in symbolic or mystical language, referring to higher realities that require deeper interpretation beyond what is immediately obvious. For this reason, we need to rely on the work of those who have either accessed now-lost sources or uncovered these teachings through the same intuitive methods that first brought them to light.

The Hermetic system starts with the principle that nothing can come from nothing and recognizes that consciousness is essential to existence. From this foundation, it logically concludes that everything comes from a pure, absolute being. This being is unmanifested and unlimited but contains within it the potential to express itself. It is not just a being with life, mind, and substance—it *is* life, mind, and substance. The universe is a reflection of this divine self, showing how this being manifests itself in the material world. Some thinkers have developed new ways to apply these teachings, but they remain true to the Hermetic tradition.

However, no amount of knowledge or effort can replace the intuitive insight needed to recognize true Hermetic wisdom. Only with such insight can one grasp the genuine nature of these teachings, and it is hoped that this understanding will not be missing here. What follows is only a brief outline, as even the best attempts can offer only a glimpse of these deep truths.

The Hermetic view holds that all things are forms of consciousness, and consciousness exists in many different ways. It can be defined as the ability of something to affect or be affected by itself or something else, meaning that consciousness is the essence of everything. There are various levels of consciousness, including physical, chemical, magnetic, mental, and spiritual, with divine consciousness being the highest. All forms of consciousness come from the divine, and all will eventually return to it. This process is the essence of evolution, which is the tendency of things to return to their original state. Evolution shows that the material world is not the ultimate form of existence but is instead one step along the way.

By seeing matter as just another form of consciousness—and, in turn, a form of spirit—Hermetic thought avoids the difficulties that come with believing in two opposing forces, such as spirit and matter, as separate and conflicting. Everything is an expression of the same ultimate source, so there can be no true conflict or opposition. What we call unconsciousness is simply a lower form of consciousness, reduced to its smallest degree but still present. Total unconsciousness is non-existence, just as darkness is the absence of light. Consciousness, however limited, always has a positive existence, while non-existence is only the absence of being.

The many expressions of consciousness, whether on different levels or in different forms on the same level, all follow the same underlying law. This law reveals the unity of the divine mind, which exists eternally, independent of its manifestations. As stated in the "Divine Pymander": "He does not need to be revealed, for He exists eternally. He is not created or born but remains unseen and unmanifested. Yet, by making all things visible, He appears in all things and through all things, especially in those who seek Him."

The unity of being also establishes a principle of correspondence between all levels of existence. The larger universe mirrors the smaller individual, just as the individual reflects the divine. "Man on earth," says "The Key," "is a mortal god, while the heavenly god is an immortal man." However, the book clarifies that this description only applies to those who possess higher spiritual awareness. Those who lack this awareness are not yet fully human but only have the potential to become so.

The teachings avoid the mistake of attributing human qualities to the divine by explaining that divinity is not life, mind, or substance itself but the source of these things. Ignorance of the divine is described as the greatest evil, but God cannot be found in the external world. Instead, the search for the divine must take place within oneself. To truly know, one must first fully *be*. This means developing awareness of all the different levels of one's being and becoming a complete person. The deepest truths belong to the spirit, which is the pure essence of being. Existence is simply the outward expression of that essence.

Since a person can only recognize in the external world what they already have within themselves, spiritual awareness is necessary to perceive spiritual truths. To understand the divine, a person must first become spiritual within.

"The natural man," as the apostle Paul says, following the teachings of both the Hermetists and the Kabbalists, "cannot understand the things of the Spirit, nor can he know them, for they are understood spiritually." This means they can only be grasped through the spiritual part within a person. As a person develops this spiritual awareness, they become a tool for knowledge, capable of discovering deep truths, including the highest truths. At that point, they move from being "agnostic," or unaware of true knowledge, to being "Gnostic," which means having knowledge of both themselves and God, and understanding that both are deeply connected.

The fact that today's world often embraces agnosticism only shows how immature its understanding is. The philosophy of this time reflects the views of people who may be highly intelligent but are still underdeveloped in their spiritual awareness. Because of this, they have not yet reached their full human potential, which requires growth on the spiritual plane. Lacking this higher awareness, they mistake the outward appearance of a person for their true self, assuming that satisfying physical desires will benefit the person, even if such actions harm their deeper humanity.

The knowledge provided by Gnosis helps lift people out of this spiritual darkness. It gives them the essential understanding that all divine teachings aim to provide: a clear understanding of who they truly are. It shows, with certainty, that moral laws are supreme and that it is impossible to gain anything good by doing wrong or to escape the consequences of one's actions. Trying to achieve good by doing harm only makes things worse in the long run. The idea of Karma, central to Hindu thought, is also part of Hermetic philosophy. In Hermetic teachings, this principle is represented by Adrasté, a goddess of justice. In Greek mythology, this same idea is reflected in Nemesis and Hecate. All these figures represent the unbreakable law of cause and effect, which shapes a person's future based on the actions and habits they choose to nurture in the present.

The Hermetic path to perfection—whether physical, intellectual, moral, or spiritual—is through purity. Since consciousness is not just something a person has but something they are, a person's level of awareness depends on how pure they are. Perfect purity allows for complete understanding, even to the point of seeing God, as taught in the gospels. In the same way, a person's power increases with their purity. A fully developed Hermetist, someone who has mastered this knowledge, becomes a magian—a person of great power. Such a person can perform acts that seem miraculous, not just physically but also intellectually, morally, and spiritually, all through the strength of their will. However, the secret of this power is purity, and the only motivation behind it is love. The power they use comes from spirit, and spirit becomes more powerful the purer it is. Pure spirit, at its highest level, is God.

The miracles performed by a magian differ from those of a magician because they are truly the work of God—the divine power within the person. A key part of Hermetic knowledge is the use of intuition. Through intuition, a person turns inward and connects with their true, eternal self—the soul—and gains access to the knowledge it has gathered over countless lifetimes. This approach does not dismiss the role of the intellect, which also needs to be developed as a partner to intuition. These two aspects of the mind—intellect and intuition—are like complements, working together like the masculine and feminine. Only when both are perfected and unified can a person achieve complete understanding. At that point, the person knows God, and to know God is to both possess and become one with God, for "the gift of God is eternal life."

One of the most important teachings in Hermetic philosophy is the idea that the soul is born into many physical bodies over time. The soul continues this cycle of rebirth until it reaches a state of spiritual growth that allows it to exist without needing a physical body. This process of transformation, called regeneration, only ends when the soul no longer needs the material world. The concept of correspondence offers a useful way to understand this process. Just as the body sheds its outer layers—such as skin, feathers, or hair—the soul also leaves behind many physical bodies over time.

The law of gravity, which governs the physical world, also applies to the spiritual world. A person's spiritual state determines the level at which their soul exists, just as the density of a physical object determines how it behaves. The soul must release the attachment that draws it into physical existence before it can move beyond the need for a body. The death of the body does not necessarily mean that the soul has overcome this pull toward material life, so the soul may still be drawn back to earth in another body. However, when the soul returns, it does so without the magnetic or "astral" body that forms the outer personality. Only the soul itself continues its journey, evolving through each lifetime toward greater spiritual awareness.

The idea of transmigration, or the soul's journey through many lifetimes, is central to Hermetic, Kabbalistic, and Hindu teachings. It also runs through the Bible in hidden ways, showing up in the conversation between Jesus and Nicodemus, where Jesus speaks about being "born again." Although Jesus emphasizes spiritual rebirth, this process requires multiple lifetimes to provide the experiences necessary for spiritual growth. As Swedenborg explained, regeneration must begin while a person is still in the body and must reach a certain level before the soul can move beyond needing a physical body. Spiritual growth cannot be completed in a single lifetime. Without many lifetimes to make this process possible, the message of the gospel would not offer salvation but would instead guarantee failure for most people.

In Hermetic teachings, what Christianity calls the "forgiveness of sins" is tied to the process of inner transformation. Each person carries the potential for this transformation within them, but they must actively participate in their own spiritual growth. Through this process, they become a "new creation," born not from physical matter but from "water and spirit." This means their soul and spirit are purified, becoming divine. When a person achieves this higher state of being, they are said to be born of the "Virgin Mary" and the Holy Spirit.

The Hermetic system stands apart from other mystical traditions because it views nature and the body with joy and reverence, rather than disgust. While some other systems see the body and its functions as impure or sinful, Hermeticism sees them as part of divine truth. The relationship between the sexes is honored, symbolizing the highest spiritual mysteries, and fulfilling these relationships is considered a duty. In some lifetimes, these experiences are essential for a person's complete development and initiation. This appreciation of life's beauty aligns Hermetic thought with Greek philosophy and sets it apart from more pessimistic Eastern views.

A true Hermetist sees divine presence everywhere—in every part of nature, just as the prophet Jonah found God even in the belly of a whale. Ignorance of God is viewed as the greatest evil. This belief is why Hermetic teachings promote a vegetarian lifestyle, as described in the "Asclepios." Human beings are not naturally designed to eat meat. Their physical structure shows that they thrive best on plant-based foods, which cleanse and rebuild the body. Eating flesh not only blocks the development of intuition, the key to spiritual insight, but also dulls a person's sensitivity to violence. Failing to be disturbed by killing for food reveals a lack of spiritual awareness.

The goal of the Hermetist is not simply to escape from life, as if existence were something evil. Instead, the goal is to become a clear instrument for perceiving the divine presence in every part of existence. Any pessimism found in Hermetic texts, such as the "Divine Pymander," reflects only the imperfections of existence compared to the perfection of divine being. Hermeticism surpasses other mystical systems by valuing both sexes equally. Although the story of the Fall originates from Hermetic teachings, it is meant to be understood symbolically, not literally. It was never intended to place blame on any person or gender. Instead, the Fall represents a deep truth about divine reality. Sadly, this story has often been used to justify unfair and cruel treatment of women— attitudes that come from primitive and undeveloped sources, not from true spiritual understanding.

Throughout history, it becomes clear that the solutions to life's greatest questions—about human nature and how to live—can be found in the teachings and practices of the Hermetic system. Free inquiry, when pursued without prejudice or narrow thinking, naturally leads to the truths revealed by Hermeticism. These teachings are based on real, lived experiences of the soul, which gains deeper understanding through intuition.

Hermetic philosophy is a triumph of both free thought and religious faith. It encourages exploration of both the physical world and the spiritual realm. In Hermeticism, God is seen as the source of all being. Nature serves as a way for God to reveal Himself, and the human soul—refined and perfected through experience—becomes a unique expression of the divine.

AN INTRODUCTION TO THE VIRGIN OF THE WORLD

The mystical title of the well-known Hermetic fragment that opens this volume, "Koré Kosmou," or "The Kosmic Virgin," reveals the deep connection between the ancient wisdom-religions and the teachings of Catholic Christianity. In the Eleusinian Mysteries, the name Koré was used to address Persephone, the Maiden or Daughter. Interestingly, Koré is also the Greek word for the pupil of the eye. This connection becomes more meaningful when we consider that, in a conversation between Isis, the Moon-goddess and guide of initiates, and Horos, she compares the physical eye's layers to the soul's coverings. Just as the eye's pupil brings light to the body, the soul brings awareness and understanding to a person.

In this Hermetic parable, Persephone, or Koré, symbolizes the soul. Her descent from the divine realm into the material world is a key theme. Some scholars have also noted that the Hindu goddess Parasu-pani, also known as Gorée, shares a similar role, suggesting a deeper connection between these traditions. The Greek Mysteries focused on two primary themes: the story of Persephone's descent and return, and the life, death, and rebirth of Dionysos-Zagreus. In these teachings, Persephone represents the soul, while Dionysos symbolizes the spirit.

The Hermetic doctrine explains that both the universe and human beings have a fourfold nature. Two parts of this nature—spirit and soul—are eternal, while the other two—the lower mind and the physical body—are temporary. The spirit and soul, viewed as masculine and feminine forces, remain unchanged through all cycles of reincarnation, while the mind and body are new with each life. Dionysos, the spirit, is said to have a divine origin, being born from Zeus and the immaculate Virgin Koré-Persephone, who is the daughter of Demeter, known as the "Mother" in the Mysteries.

Koré has two aspects to her nature. As the daughter of Zeus and Demeter, she is pure and divine. However, as the wife of Hades in the underworld, she is connected to the realms of sorrow and decay. This duality reflects the nature of the soul, which remains pure and invulnerable in its essence, yet appears to fall and become stained in the material world. The symbol of the soul in Hermetic teachings is water, also called Maria. Water, though it can appear dirty or polluted, always retains its true purity beneath the surface. When purified through distillation, it leaves all impurities behind and emerges clear and pure once again. In the same way, the soul is always pure at its core, no matter how stained it might seem during its journey through life.

The story of the Kosmic Virgin reflects the soul's journey through existence. The soul moves between two states: an outward journey into the material world, which represents its "fall," and an inward return to its divine origin. Although Koré comes from a heavenly realm, she is more connected to earthly life than her son, Dionysos. As the Mysteries teach, Persephone dwells both above, in the inaccessible places of the divine Mother, and below, with Pluto, where she governs earthly matters and sustains life throughout the universe.

This dual nature of spirit and soul is also central to Hindu philosophy, where the spirit is called Atman. The Upanishads, a key part of Hindu esoteric teachings, focus entirely on understanding this concept.

The concept of Atman is described as self-sustaining, unified, eternal, unchanging, and incorruptible. It exists independently of Karma—the idea that actions shape one's character and destiny— and gaining full awareness of Atman frees a person from the cycle of Karma. Atman is also all-seeing, and as the Mantras teach, "He who sees the universe within his own Atman and his Atman within the universe knows no hatred."

In the Kabbalah, the soul's journey is symbolized by Eve. The soul begins by turning away from divine unity and becoming restless in matter, unable to stay still, as resting seems like death. This moment is reflected in the Greek myth where Persephone leaves the heavens, lured by desire, and falls under Hades' power. Thomas Taylor explains this descent as the soul abandoning its higher, divine life. In the story, Jupiter sends Venus to tempt Persephone from her peaceful retreat, with Diana and Minerva accompanying her to prevent any suspicion. They find Persephone weaving a scarf for her mother, depicting the chaos and creation of the world.

Venus represents desire, which sneaks into the soul even in heavenly realms. Minerva symbolizes reason, while Diana stands for nature. As Persephone wanders from her retreat to gather flowers, surrounded by nymphs symbolizing the cycle of life and birth, she becomes captivated by the beauty of the material world. The soul, in the same way, becomes enchanted by the world of form and sensation. As soon as she steps outside her retreat, Pluto rises from the earth and seizes her, dragging her into the underworld. This reflects the soul's descent into the darkness of material existence, where it is united with the body.

Homer's "Hymn to Ceres" also describes this event, with Persephone saying, "I was joyfully gathering flowers—the crocus, iris, hyacinth, and narcissus—when the earth opened, and the powerful king carried me down to the underworld, despite my cries." This story mirrors the biblical tale of Eve, who, drawn by the beauty of the tree's fruit, eats it and is cast into sorrow. God tells her, "I will increase your pain in childbirth, and your desire will be for your husband, who will rule over you."

Plato's allegory in "Phaedrus" further explains this fall, comparing the body to a chariot pulling the soul down into earthly existence. The soul struggles under the weight of material life, which clouds the mind and reason. This condition, Plato explains, traps the soul in the body, similar to prisoners chained in a cave who mistake shadows for reality. Life on earth is described as a form of imprisonment—a dreamlike exile from the soul's true home.

In the "Koré Kosmou," we read that souls, upon learning they would be trapped in physical bodies, sighed and cried out to the heavens. They lamented, "Oh, what sorrow and heartache to leave behind these vast splendors, the sacred realm, and all the glory of the blessed gods, only to be cast down into these miserable and wretched dwellings! We will no longer gaze upon the radiant heavens!" This sorrowful cry brings to mind Eve's lament when she was exiled from the beautiful paradise of Eden.

Just as the soul falls into this sorrowful state, she is eventually rescued and restored to the divine realm. This rescue happens through the coming of a savior, symbolized here by Osiris, the figure of the "Man Regenerate." Osiris, a divine being, is often represented by different names in various stories, but the meaning behind each is the same. Osiris is the equivalent of Jesus in Christian doctrine—the supreme initiate and "Captain of Salvation." Alongside his divine partner, Osiris is guided in all things by Hermes, known as the messenger of the gods. Hermes is seen as the conductor of souls from darkness, representing divine understanding and reason. In Platonic philosophy, Hermes embodies "nous," the higher mind, and the mystical "Spirit of Christ."

Since the ability to understand sacred things and interpret them comes from Hermes, the name Hermes is connected to all hidden knowledge and divine revelation. Those with such knowledge are known as "divines," meaning they understand the mysteries of heaven. This is why the apostle John, who wrote the Book of Revelation, is often called the "beloved" of Christ. Hermes is recognized as the messenger of the gods, descending to the deepest realms of the underworld to guide souls upward and ascending beyond the heavens to bring wisdom. Understanding must explore both the heights and the depths, for nothing can remain hidden from it. Only by exploring both the spiritual and material realms can a person fully grasp divine truths.

26

The Greeks, with their joyful and lighthearted nature, added humor and playfulness even to their sacred stories. They called Hermes a thief, hinting at the power of the mind to claim everything for its own understanding. When the myths say that Hermes stole the girdle of Venus, the tools of Vulcan, the thunder of Zeus, and the cattle of Apollo, they mean that even the greatest gifts of the gods are within reach of the mind when it seeks knowledge wisely. As the companion of the sun, Hermes opens the gates of heaven, revealing spiritual light and life. He serves as a mediator between the physical and spiritual worlds, initiating seekers into the sacred mysteries that lead to eternal life.

The symbolic tools carried by Hermes reflect the powers of the mind. His rod represents the wisdom of the magian, his wings signify the courage of the adventurer, his sword embodies the will of the hero, and his cap shows the discretion of the wise. Those initiated into Hermes' teachings recognize no authority but the mind itself. They follow no earthly master, embracing the freedom of true understanding. As scripture says, "Where the Spirit of the Lord is, there is liberty." One advisor of John Inglesant put it this way: "Follow no man; there is nothing of greater value in the world than the Divine Light—follow it."

Lactantius, in his writings, says that Hermes taught how knowing God frees a person from the control of demons and fate. Fate, in this sense, is tied to the power of the stars, which control both the cosmos and the inner life of a person. In Greek mythology, the many-eyed Argos, who represents the watchful power of the stars, was outwitted and slain by Hermes. This story teaches that those who gain the secret knowledge of Hermes rise above fate and break free from the endless cycles of destiny. To know God is to overcome death and conquer the forces that hold one back. Understanding the source of illusion allows a person to transcend it.

The path to God is blocked by layers of deception, ruled by the seven astral powers. These spheres of illusion stand between the soul and God. Beyond them lie the nine celestial realms, where, according to the Mysteries, Demeter once searched in vain for her lost daughter, Persephone. Persephone had fallen into the material world, placing her under the control of the planetary rulers, symbolized by Hecate, the goddess of fate. On the tenth day of her search, Demeter encountered Hecate, the three-formed goddess of karma and retribution, who revealed what had happened to Persephone. From that moment, Hecate became Persephone's constant companion.

This story holds deep meaning. The soul is free from fate until it enters the material world. Fate begins with the soul's involvement in time and physical existence. In the sevenfold astral spheres, the moon symbolizes fate, presenting both a benevolent and a harsh face.

Under her kinder aspect, the Moon is Artemis, reflecting the divine light of Phœbos to the soul. In her harsher form, she is Hecate, the Avenger, dark-faced and three-headed, swift like a horse, sharp as a dog, and fierce as a lion. In this form, she hunts guilty souls from one life to the next, ensuring justice with relentless precision, outmaneuvering even death. For pure and innocent souls, however, the Moon offers a guiding light. As Artemis, she protects virgins—those souls untouched by the pull of the material world. In this role, the Moon becomes an initiator, like Isis, lighting the soul's inner chamber and bringing wisdom through a favorable destiny. With each lifetime, such souls grow more enlightened and become prophetic, even divine.

On the other hand, to those corrupted by evil, the Moon appears as Hecate, bringing nightmares and dark warnings of misfortune. These souls fear the power of the Moon, sensing the misfortune they are creating for their future selves. According to the Kabbalah, the Tree of Good and Evil is rooted in Malchuth, the Moon. While some say that Karma is unique to Hindu thought, it appears just as clearly in the Hebrew, Greek, and Christian teachings. The Greeks called it Fate, while in Christianity, it is known as Original Sin—the burden that all mortals carry. Only the "Mother of God" is exempt, the "immaculate virgin" through whose child the world is redeemed. As the Church sings, "As a lily among thorns, so is the Beloved among the daughters of Adam. You are all beautiful, O Beloved, and there is no stain within you; your name, O Mary, is like oil poured out, and the virgins love you greatly."

In Persephone or Koré, the "Virgin of the World," we see the soul. In Isis, the guiding initiator, we see the teacher. Isis, like Koré, is both a virgin and a mother. In her philosophical role, the Egyptian Isis is equivalent to Artemis of Ephesus, the Greek goddess symbolizing nature's power to nourish and create. She was called the "eternal maid of heaven," and her priests were eunuchs. Her statue in the grand temple of Ephesus portrayed her with many breasts, symbolizing abundance. The black skin of some depictions, such as the "Black Virgin," represents the hidden and mysterious nature of the forces that shape destiny. These forces may seem random to those who lack understanding, but they follow deeper spiritual laws.

In art, Artemis is often depicted as a huntress with hounds, representing the relentless forces of nature. She is also shown as the Moon goddess, wearing a long veil and a crescent crown, or as a many-breasted mother, carrying a torch. The Romans knew her as Diana, and it is by this name that the Artemis of Ephesus is mentioned in the Christian scriptures. Like Artemis and Diana, Isis embodies the hidden power of nature—Fate, which manifests as fortune, retribution, and destiny. The Kabbalists represent this power with Malchuth, the Moon, while Hindu philosophy calls it Karma. Artemis' hounds symbolize the natural forces that pursue the soul through each lifetime, ensuring that every soul faces the results of its actions.

In the story of Actaeon, the hero ignores the sacredness of fate and disrespects the law of Karma. As punishment, he is torn apart by his own hounds, symbolizing how one's own actions can turn against them. Similarly, initiates of Isis wore masks with dog heads during processions, showing their understanding of how closely fate is tied to the soul's journey. The Moon, linked with Karma, represents the force that draws souls through cycles of birth and rebirth. Proclus, a Greek philosopher, explained that Diana, or Artemis, governs the process by which all things are born into the natural world and extends her power even to the underworld.

This view perfectly describes the role of Isis, showing how the Moon, as the force of Karma, drives the ongoing cycle of life and follows the soul even into realms of purification after death. In the Orphic Hymn to Nature, the goddess is shown standing on a wheel that she spins endlessly, representing the eternal movement of fate. In another hymn, Fortune, identified with Diana, is invoked as the goddess who controls destiny.

Proclus adds that the Moon is not only the cause of nature for mortals but also a reflection of a deeper source—the fountain of life itself. As Thomas Taylor explains, this fountain consists of three main sources within the Demiurge, or creator of the world: the fountain of souls, personified by Hera; the fountain of virtues, represented by Athena; and the fountain of nature, embodied by Artemis. Taylor further illustrates this concept with a passage from Apuleius' "Metamorphoses," in which the Moon speaks: "Behold, Lucius, moved by your prayers, I am here. I am Nature, the mother of all things, ruler of the elements, the beginning of time, the highest among gods and goddesses. I control the bright heavens, the winds of the sea, and the silent darkness of the underworld. Though my essence is one, all the earth honors me by many names and worships me through many rites. Those blessed by the rising sun—the Ethiopians, Aryans, and Egyptians, who possess ancient wisdom—know me as Queen Isis."

The hymn continues with praise: "The gods above honor you, and even those below bow to your power. You set the world in motion, guide the sun's light, and rule the entire universe. The stars obey your will, the gods celebrate you, time flows by your command, and the elements serve you."

This understanding follows naturally when we consider that the divine fountain of Nature exists within the Demiurgus and serves as the pattern for the nature we observe in the Moon and throughout the material world. Knowing this, it is easy to understand why the writer of the Hermetic text chose Isis to represent the soul's origin, journey, and destiny. Isis plays a unique role in guiding the soul through its existence, overseeing its path. If Demeter, the divine intelligence, is the true mother of Koré, then Isis acts as the foster-mother, taking over as soon as the soul enters the material world. Once the soul begins its earthly existence, Isis directs it and determines its fate. This is why some myths equate Isis with Demeter, adjusting Isis's role to match the story of Demeter's grief, as told in the Eleusinian Mysteries.

This blending of roles becomes clear when we understand the Hermetic teachings. Isis, whether she appears as Artemis (good fortune) or Hekate (bad fortune), governs and enlightens the soul while it is still bound by nature and time. Meanwhile, Demeter represents the heavenly source from which the soul originates. Demeter's concern is not with the soul's exile in the physical world but with its eventual return to the divine realm. In harmony with this idea, Isis is depicted both as the wife and the mother of Osiris, the savior of humankind. Osiris, the inner sun of the human soul, reflects the cosmic Dionysos, or Son of God, just as the soul mirrors the greater universe. This is why some myths merge Isis with Demeter and Osiris with Dionysos, placing Osiris at the center of the Bacchic Mysteries.

The Hermetic writings present three levels of divine expression. First, there is the supreme, eternal God, who exists beyond all manifestation. Second is the only-begotten God, the expression of the divine within the universe. Third is the divine presence within humanity, embodied by Osiris, the redeemer. Inscriptions found on the walls of the Temple of the Sun at Philae and the gate at Medinet-Abou read, "He made all things, and without Him, nothing exists." These words, later used in the Gospel of John to describe the Word of God, show the connection between Osiris, the inner light of humanity, and the divine principle of creation.

Osiris, the inner sun within each person, is a reflection of the greater cosmic sun. The soul, through its experiences in time and physical existence, gives birth to this inner light. This connection explains why Osiris, the force of renewal within each individual, is closely linked to Isis, who guides the soul's growth. Through her influence, events and conditions shape the soul's development, preparing it for transformation. Isis symbolizes the hidden force that drives evolution forward, while Osiris represents the highest potential of humanity, the ideal self toward which all growth is directed.

• • •

The Virgin of The World

PART 1

After speaking, Isis gave Horos a sweet drink, the gift of immortality, which is granted by the gods to souls. Then, she began her sacred teaching. She explained that the heavens, crowned with stars, exist above all of creation, complete and lacking nothing. All of nature must be perfected by what is above, as the order of the universe flows from the higher to the lower realms. This order cannot begin from below and move upward. The higher mysteries always rule over the lower ones. Celestial order governs the earthly order, being eternal and beyond death. The things of earth feel fear before the eternal beauty and permanence of the heavens.

The heavens, with their glorious sights, display the majesty of a divine power not yet fully understood. The night sky, though less bright than the sun, reveals hidden mysteries that move in harmony, quietly guiding life on earth through unseen forces. Before the Divine Architect revealed Himself, the universe was full of fear and uncertainty. Ignorance surrounded everything. But when He chose to reveal Himself, He filled the gods with love

34

and poured into them the wisdom contained within His being. This gave them the desire to seek, the will to find, and the power to restore what had been lost.

This great awakening did not happen among mortals, for humanity had not yet come into existence. Instead, it took place within the universal Soul, reflecting the mysteries of the heavens. This universal Soul was Hermes, the cosmic thought. He observed the universe, understood its nature, and revealed what he had discovered. Hermes wrote down these truths, but he kept many hidden, alternating between speaking and remaining silent so that these secrets would continue to be sought throughout time. He instructed the other gods to follow his lead, and then he returned to the stars. Hermes passed his knowledge to his son, Tat, and later to Asclepios, the son of Imouthè, guided by Pan and Hephaistos.

Hermes explained to those around him that he did not reveal the complete knowledge to his son because of his youth. But I, Isis, with my eyes that see the hidden truths of the universe, witnessed these events. And I saw those who, through divine guidance, were granted a perfect understanding of the mysteries of the heavens.

It is important, my son, that you hear the words of Hermes when he sealed his sacred books. "O holy books of the Immortals," he said, "within you are written the remedies that grant eternal life. Remain hidden from those who dwell in this realm until a time comes when souls, worthy of your knowledge, will be born under the ancient heavens."

Hermes then wrapped his books and returned to his place among the stars, leaving his teachings hidden for a time. Nature remained barren until those ordained to observe the heavens sought divine help. They prayed to the Creator, saying, "Please consider what is and what must still come to be." The Creator smiled and commanded Nature to bring forth life. With His voice, the feminine aspect of creation emerged in perfect beauty, leaving the gods amazed. The great Ancestor poured an elixir over Nature, making her fruitful. He declared, "Let heaven be filled with all things, along with the air and the ether." And it was so.

Nature, reflecting on her purpose, realized that she must not stray from the Creator's command. She joined with Labor to bring forth a beautiful daughter, whom she named Invention. The Creator gave Invention life and charged her with shaping creation. He filled the universe with mysteries and entrusted Invention to oversee them. Not wishing for the heavens to remain idle, the Creator filled the upper world with spirits, ensuring that all regions of existence were active. Using sacred knowledge, He formed these beings by mixing His essence with an intellectual flame, along with other elements through hidden means.

From this mixture, a substance more refined and pure than the original elements emerged. It was transparent, visible only to the divine Artist. This new creation reached perfection, immune to both fire and cold, stable in its form and nature. The Creator named this essence Self-Consciousness. From it, He formed countless souls, carefully choosing the finest parts of the mixture for His purpose. Although the souls were not identical, the finest ones were animated by divine motion and set apart from the rest.

The Creator arranged the souls into layers, each more refined than the one beneath it, until sixty degrees were completed. Though the souls differed in rank, they all shared the same eternal essence, determined by the Creator alone. He placed them in their rightful places in the order of nature, instructing them to turn the wheel of life with wisdom and joy, fulfilling the divine plan.

Summoning these souls to the realms of ether, the Creator spoke to them: "O souls, my beloved children, formed from my breath and care, created by my hands to serve my universe, hear my law: Do not abandon the place I have prepared for you. Your home is the heavens, adorned with stars and thrones of virtue.

If you go against my command, I swear by my sacred breath, the same life-giving essence from which you were created, and by my creative hands, that I will quickly forge chains to bind you and cast you into punishment." After speaking these words, God combined the remaining elements—earth and water—into a new form. Using different, powerful words, He breathed life and motion into the liquid protoplasm, thickening it into a pliable material. From this, He shaped living beings in human form. He gave the remaining substance to the divine souls dwelling near the stars, known as the Sacred Genii, and instructed them: "Continue my work, my children, born of my nature. Use what I have left and shape beings in your own image. I will provide models."

God took the signs of the Zodiac and arranged them to guide creation, placing the animals after the human forms. He released the generative forces for all living beings, then withdrew, promising that every creation would carry an invisible breath and a reproductive essence so that life could continue without needing to be created from scratch.

"What did the souls do then, my Mother?" asked Horos. Isis replied, "They studied the material given to them, contemplating and admiring the Father's work. They sought to understand its components, though it was not easy to uncover. Fearing the Father's anger, they focused on following His commands. They used the lightest part of the protoplasm to create birds. As the mixture thickened, they formed quadrupeds, and with the densest part, supported by water, they created fish. The heaviest and coldest portions were used to make reptiles. Proud of their work, the souls began to disobey the divine law. They could not bear to stay in one place, restless in their pursuit of change, as stillness seemed like death to them."

Hermes told me that their disobedience did not escape the notice of the Lord. He decided to punish the souls and prepare chains to restrain them. To correct them, He shaped the human body—a blend of mortal and immortal elements. God summoned Hermes and said, "Soul of my soul, thought of my thought, how long must the world remain barren and without praise? How much longer will creation lie unfinished? Bring the gods before me." At His command, all the gods gathered. "Look upon the earth and everything below," God told them. When the gods gazed down, they understood His will.

When He asked what each god could offer to the new human race, the Sun spoke first: "I will illuminate them." The Moon followed, promising to bring enlightenment, along with Fear, Silence, Sleep, and Memory, which she had already created. Kronos offered Justice and Necessity. Zeus declared, "To prevent endless wars, I will bestow Fortune, Hope, and Peace." Ares proclaimed that he had already fathered Conflict, Zeal, and Ambition. Aphrodite eagerly added, "I will gift humans with Desire, Joy, and Laughter, so that the burdens placed upon their souls may not weigh too heavily."

The other gods welcomed Aphrodite's offer. Hermes then said, "I will grant humans Wisdom, Temperance, Persuasion, and Truth, and I will remain closely allied with Invention. I will protect the lives of those born under my signs, for the Creator has entrusted me with the Zodiac signs that govern Knowledge and Intelligence. I will assist whenever the stars align with the natural forces of these individuals."

The Lord rejoiced at the gods' offerings and decreed that the human race would be created. Hermes continued, "I sought the proper materials for this task and prayed to the Lord for guidance. He ordered the souls to release the leftover protoplasm. However, when I received it, it had dried up, so I added an excess of water to soften it. I ensured the new form would remain flexible and fragile, balancing intelligence with vulnerability. Once my work was complete, it was beautiful, and I rejoiced in what I had made. I called upon the Lord to witness my creation. He looked upon it and approved, ordering the souls to inhabit the forms."

The souls, upon learning of their fate, were filled with dread. Isis continued, "These words shook me deeply. Listen closely, my son Horos, for I share a great mystery with you. Our ancestor Kamephes received this knowledge from Hermes, who recorded all things. Kamephes passed it to me when I underwent the initiation of the black veil. Now I pass it to you, my beloved and extraordinary child."

Isis described the souls' reaction when they learned they would be bound to physical bodies. Some sighed and lamented, like wild animals suddenly captured and forced into servitude, rebelling against their captors. Others hissed like serpents or cried out in despair, looking helplessly from the heights of heaven to the depths below.

One soul cried, "Great Heaven, source of our birth, pure air, sacred breath of God, and you, shining stars, the unceasing light of the Sun and Moon—our brothers in the heavens—what sorrow awaits us! Must we leave these vast, radiant spaces, this sacred realm, and all the splendors of the divine world? Are we to be cast down into miserable, wretched places? What crime have we committed to deserve this punishment? What terrible sin have we, poor souls, committed to merit such suffering?"

Behold the sorrowful future that lies ahead—to tend to the needs of a fragile and fleeting body! No longer will our eyes perceive the souls of divine beings clearly. Through these clouded, earthly lenses, we will barely glimpse, with longing, our ancestral home in the heavens. There will be times when we won't see it at all. This tragic fate denies us the ability to see directly; we must rely on external light to see. Our eyes become mere windows, not true vision. And our suffering will deepen when we hear the winds breathing freely in the air—winds that we can no longer join. Our breath will be trapped, not in the wide, open world, but within the narrow prison of our own chests! Yet, O Master and Father, who cast us down from such a high place to this lowly state, set a limit to our suffering! Do not become indifferent to your creation. Let our punishment have an end, and give us a final message before we lose sight of the shining realms above!

This plea from the Souls was answered, my son Horos, for the Lord was present. Seated on the throne of Truth, He spoke: "Souls, you will be governed by Desire and Necessity. They will be your rulers and guides after Me. As long as you remain pure, you will live in the heavens. But if some of you are found guilty, you will dwell within mortal bodies. If your faults are minor, you will return to the heavens after being freed from the flesh. But those who commit serious wrongs, who abandon their true purpose, will not return to the heavens nor inhabit human bodies—they will enter the bodies of animals without reason."

It has been debated whether the Hermetic teachings support the idea of reincarnation into lower life forms. I believe they do align with this belief, without contradiction. The Divine Pymander states that if a human soul continues to act wickedly, "it will neither taste immortality nor partake in the good, but will be pulled back into creeping creatures; this is the fate of an evil soul." However, Hermes clarifies that a truly human soul—one containing the divine Mind—cannot fall this low, even if it has strayed. As long as the soul holds the divine fire within, it remains human, and such a soul is compared not to animals but to beings above, even to gods. Yet, if a soul falls so far that this inner flame is extinguished, it becomes dark and forsaken, no longer human. "Such a soul," says Hermes, "has lost the Mind and should not be called human."

This teaching emphasizes that a human soul cannot enter the body of a mindless creature, nor can it become something less than human unless it loses its divine essence. When a soul sinks to this low state, it gravitates toward creatures that match its nature. After its purification, however, the soul may awaken and say, "I will return to my Father." Some Rabbis have even suggested that this is the hidden meaning of the parable of the prodigal son, where the swine symbolize lust and base desires. The Hermetic view aligns with the Kabbalah and the teachings of Apollonius of Tyana on this point.

After addressing the souls, the Lord breathed upon them and said, "Your destiny is not left to chance. If you act wrongly, things will go badly for you; if you act wisely, they will improve. I, not another, will be your witness and judge. Your suffering in physical bodies is the result of your past mistakes. Each rebirth will be different, as I have already told you. Death will be a gift, restoring you to a better state. But if you act against My will, your judgment will be clouded. You will mistake suffering for fortune and fear happiness as if it were a curse.

Those among you who act with justice will rise closer to the divine in future lives. They will become wise rulers, true philosophers, visionary leaders, healers of plants, talented musicians, knowledgeable astronomers, insightful prophets, and servants of wisdom. These are noble roles. Just as the eagle does not harm its kind and protects the weak with justice, or the lion, who tirelessly performs great deeds in his mortal body, so too are the wise uplifted. The dragon, who is powerful, gentle, and a friend to man, embodies divine traits, and the dolphin, who saves drowning people without devouring them, shows kindness even as the most voracious sea creature."

After saying these things, the Lord returned to His incorruptible, unmanifested state. Then, my son Horos, a mighty Spirit arose from the earth. He had no physical form, yet was filled with wisdom and strength. Although fearsome, this Spirit knew what he sought and observed the human form with admiration, for it was both beautiful and dignified. He noticed the souls about to enter their bodies and asked, "What are these beings, Hermes, Secretary of the Gods?"

"These are men," replied Hermes.

The Spirit remarked, "It is risky to create men with such keen sight, quick tongues, and sharp hearing, allowing them to sense things not meant for them. They will have hands skilled enough to grasp anything. Is it wise to leave them free from care? These creatures, who will explore every corner of the earth, study plants and stones, and even dissect themselves to learn how they are made? They will cut down forests to cross seas in search of each other, and they will pursue the secrets of nature to the highest heavens. They will seek the edges of night and try to extend their power over the elements themselves. If they are free from hardship, fear, and anxiety, nothing will stop them—not even the heavens. Teach them desire and hope, so they may also know fear and failure. Let their souls struggle with love and longing, sometimes fulfilled, sometimes not, so that even success will lead them toward misfortune. Let them face sickness and suffering, breaking their desires and humbling their hearts."

Do you feel sorrow, Horos, hearing this story? Does it surprise you to learn about the hardships awaiting humanity? What you will hear next is even more troubling. Hermes approved the Spirit's words and decided to follow his advice.

"O Momos," he said, "the divine breath that fills all things will not fail in its purpose! The Master of the universe has entrusted me to oversee His creation. The deity with the all-seeing eye, Adrastia, will watch and guide every event. As for me, I will design a mysterious tool—one that is precise and unchanging, a law that will govern everything from birth to destruction and bind all created things together. This tool will rule over the earth and everything in it."

The Lord then summoned the assembly of the gods. They gathered, and He addressed them, saying: "You gods, who possess an eternal, unchanging nature and the power to sustain the harmony of the universe, how much longer shall we reign over an invisible world? How long will creation remain hidden from the light of the sun and moon? Let us each take our place in the universe and end this stagnant state. Let us transform chaos into an ancient tale, unbelievable to those who come after us. Begin your great work, and I will guide you."

With these words, the cosmic order, which had been hidden, revealed itself. The heavens appeared in all their splendor, and the earth, once unstable, grew firm under the sun's radiance, showing forth its hidden riches. In God's eyes, everything was beautiful, even what seemed unpleasant to mortals, for everything followed the divine laws. God rejoiced, seeing His creation full of life and movement, and with His hands He gathered the treasures of nature.

"Take these," He said, "O sacred earth, take these, you who will be the mother of all things. From now on, let nothing be lacking to you." Opening His divine hands, He poured these treasures into the heart of the universe. Yet, the embodied souls, ashamed of their fate, sought to rival the gods. Proud of their noble origin, they boasted of being equals to the gods and rebelled. In their rebellion, humans became their instruments, leading to conflicts and civil wars. The strong oppressed the weak, and both the living and the dead were cast out of sacred places.

The elements, witnessing these horrors, went before the Lord to complain about the cruelty of mankind. The fire spoke first, saying, "O Master, Creator of this new world, You whose name is revered by both gods and men, how long will You allow human life to remain without divine guidance? Reveal Yourself to the world that cries out for You. Bring peace to end their savage ways. Give life its laws and night its oracles. Let happy omens fill all things. Let people fear divine judgment, so they no longer sin. Punish wrongdoing fairly, and people will avoid evil. Teach them gratitude for blessings, and I will devote my flames to pure offerings. Let the altars rise with the sweet scent of sacrifices. But now, O Master, I am polluted. The wickedness of humans forces me to burn flesh, corrupting my purity. I am no longer what I was meant to be."

The air spoke next, saying, "O Master, I am tainted by the stench of corpses. I grow poisonous and foul, forced to witness things I was never meant to see."

Then the water took its turn: "Father and Creator of all things, divine source of life, command the waters to remain pure. The rivers and seas are now used to wash away the deeds of killers and to receive their victims."

Finally, the earth spoke: "O King, Ruler of the heavens and Lord of all orbits, Master and Father of the elements, everything in creation rises and falls by Your will, and everything must return to You. But look how the wickedness of humanity spreads across me. I, who was commanded to house all beings, now bear the burden of their sins. I receive into my depths everything that dies, and this has become my shame. Your creation is empty of divine presence, and because humans revere nothing, they break every law and fill me with evil deeds. I am polluted by the remains of the dead. But I, who receive all things, ask to also receive Your presence. Grant me this grace. If You cannot come Yourself— for I could never contain You—let me receive some part of Your divine essence. Let the earth become the most honored of all the elements. Since I give all things to all beings, let me revere myself as the vessel of Your blessings."

After hearing the pleas of the elements, God filled the universe with His divine voice.

"Go forth," He said, "sacred children, worthy of your Father's greatness. Do not try to change anything, and do not deny your service to My creations. I will send a pure Being, an extension of Myself, who will examine all actions. He will be the feared and incorruptible Judge of the living, and His justice will reach even the shadows beneath the earth. In this way, each person will receive what they deserve." After this, the elements stopped their complaints and returned to their proper roles and duties.

"But how," asked Horos, "did the earth receive this gift from God?"

"I cannot reveal this birth," Isis replied. "I dare not speak of your origins, mighty Horos, for fear that future generations may discover how the Gods were created. I will only say that the Supreme God, Creator, and Builder of the world, allowed Osiris, your father, and me, the great Goddess Isis, to come to the earth for a time to bring the salvation that was promised. With our arrival, life reached its fullness. Violent and bloody wars were brought to an end. We dedicated temples to the Gods who came before us and began the practice of offerings. We provided laws, food, and clothing to mortals."

"They will read my sacred writings," said Hermes, "and divide them into two parts. Some will be kept secret, while others will be engraved on columns and obelisks for the benefit of mankind." Osiris and Isis established the first courts of justice and brought order to the world. They introduced the practice of honoring treaties and the sacred duty of making oaths. They taught the proper rites for the burial of the dead, explored the mysteries of death, and explained how the soul longs to return to the body. If this return is blocked, life itself is disrupted.

Following the teachings of Hermes, they inscribed secret messages on hidden tablets, revealing that the air is filled with spirits. Through Hermes' guidance in divine law, they became humanity's first teachers and lawgivers, introducing people to knowledge, skills, and the advantages of civilized life. They also learned from Hermes about the connections between heaven and earth, which the Creator had established, and used this knowledge to create religious rituals and sacred ceremonies. Understanding that all physical bodies are subject to decay, they developed practices of prophetic initiation. This way, prophets who raise their hands in prayer to the Gods would gain full knowledge, allowing philosophy and magic to nourish the soul and medicine to heal the body.

After completing these tasks and seeing the world reach its peak, Osiris and I were summoned back to the heavens. But we could not return without first praising the Lord, ensuring that the celestial Vision would fill the skies and that the path for a joyful ascent would open before us, for God delights in hymns."

"O Mother," said Horos, "teach me this hymn so that I may learn it too."

"Listen carefully, my son," Isis replied.

PART 2

My honored son, if you wish to know anything more, ask me. Horos replied, Revered Mother, I would like to understand how royal souls are born. Isis responded: My son Horos, this is what makes royal souls different. There are four regions in the universe, each governed by unchanging laws: heaven, the ether, the air, and the sacred earth. In heaven live the Gods, who, like everything else, follow the commands of the Creator of the universe. The stars reside in the ether and are ruled by the great fire, the sun. The souls of spirits dwell in the air, ruled by the moon. On earth are humans and animals, led by a soul that serves as their king during its time on earth.

Even the Gods themselves create the souls that are meant to become kings in the earthly world. Kings give birth to princes, and the one who embodies the most kingly nature will rise to become a greater king than others. This isn't just about ordinary kings who rule nations, but about souls destined to lead humanity, whether spiritually, intellectually, or politically. The sun, being closer to God than the moon, is stronger and greater, and the moon follows the sun both in power and rank. A king is the lowest among the Gods, yet the highest among men. While he walks on earth, his divine nature remains hidden, but there is something within him that sets him apart from others and brings him closer to the divine. His soul comes from a higher place than those of ordinary people.

There are two reasons why souls are sent to reign on earth. Some souls, having lived pure and honorable lives before, are rewarded with a chance to become divine, with royalty serving as their preparation for this higher state. Others, who committed small mistakes against the inner divine law, receive royalty as a way to correct these faults. Through the challenges and burdens of being incarnated as royalty, they ease the hardships of their earthly existence and move closer to spiritual purification.

When these souls take on a body, their experience is different from others. They remain as blessed as when they were free. The differences in the nature of these kings are not in their souls, since all are royal. Instead, it comes from the qualities of the angels and spirits that guide them. Souls chosen for these roles are always accompanied by guardians and helpers. Even though they are sent away from the divine realms, they are still treated according to their true nature.

When the angels and spirits assigned to them are warriors, the soul adopts that nature, temporarily setting aside its own. If the angels are peaceful, the soul becomes calm. If the guardians value justice, the soul takes pleasure in judging fairly. If the spirits love music, the soul finds joy in singing. If they cherish truth, the soul becomes drawn to philosophy. In this way, souls take on the qualities of their guardians. When they enter human bodies, they lose their original state and become more like the beings that helped them take form.

Horos said, Mother, your explanation is clear, but you haven't told me how noble souls are born. On earth, just as there are different roles among people, souls also have different ranks. A soul that comes from a higher realm is nobler than the rest, just as a free person is nobler than a slave. Royal and noble souls are destined to be leaders over others.

How are souls born as male or female? Horos asked. Isis answered: All souls are the same by nature because they come from the same place, created by the Creator. There are no males or females among souls—those differences exist only in physical bodies, not in spiritual beings. Some souls are more active and others are gentler, and this reflects the air that surrounds them. Souls are wrapped in airy bodies made of earth, water, air, and fire. In women, there is more coldness and moisture than heat and dryness, making their souls softer. In men, the air around the soul has more heat and dryness, which makes them more energetic and lively.

And how, my mother, are the souls of wise people born? asked Horos. Isis replied: Think of vision, which is covered by layers of tissue. If the coverings are thick, the sight is weak; if they are thin and clear, the sight is sharp. The soul, too, has coverings made of invisible air. If these coverings are fine and light, the soul becomes clear and insightful. But when the coverings are heavy and dense, the soul can only see what is nearby, like trying to see through a cloudy day.

Why is it, my mother, that the minds of people outside our sacred land seem less open than the minds of those who belong to it? Horos asked. Isis answered: The earth is positioned in the center of the universe, like a person lying on their back and looking up at the sky. The different regions of the earth correspond to different parts of this body. The earth looks to the heavens like a child looking to a father, and its changes follow the movements of the sky.

The head of the earth lies to the south, the right shoulder to the east, and the left shoulder toward the winds of Libya. The feet rest under the stars of the Bear constellation, with the right foot beneath the tail and the left foot beneath the head of the Bear. The waist aligns with the sky closest to the Bear, and the middle of the body lies under the center of the heavens. You can see proof of these connections in the way people from different places look and behave. Those who live in the south have beautiful faces and thick hair. People from the east are skilled with their hands, good in battle, and quick with a bow, using their right hands with ease. Those from the west are strong and fight with their left hands, doing with their left what others do with their right. People living beneath the Bear constellation are known for the shape and beauty of their legs. Those from places beyond the Bear, such as Italy and Greece, are admired for the beauty of their waists, which is why they often favor male companionship. That part of the body, being lighter in color, produces men with fairer skin.

The sacred land of our ancestors lies at the center of the earth. Just as the heart sits in the middle of the human body and serves as the seat of the soul, the heart of the earth gives life and wisdom to the people born from it. This is why, my son, the people of this land possess not only the same qualities that all humans share but also a higher intelligence and deeper wisdom, for they are nourished by the heart of the earth. Additionally, my son, the southern region stores the clouds, gathering them until they release the river (Nile) when the cold grows intense. Wherever these clouds gather, the air becomes heavy with mist, which not only clouds vision but also dulls the mind.

The east, my son Horos, is restless with the rising sun, just as the west stirs with the setting sun. Those who live in these regions find it difficult to maintain clear thinking. In the north, the cold hardens both body and mind. Only the central land remains calm and bright, blessing its people with tranquility. From this peaceful place, life is created and perfected. The central land stands strong against others, triumphs over them, and, like a noble ruler, shares the rewards of victory with those it has defeated.

Horos asked, Tell me more, Mother. What causes people to lose clarity, reason, or even part of their soul during long illnesses? Isis replied: Every animal connects with one or more of the elements—fire, water, earth, or air. Some creatures are closely tied to a specific element, while others are connected to two, three, or even all four. In the same way, some animals avoid certain elements. For example, insects and locusts flee from fire. Eagles, hawks, and other birds avoid water. Fish fear both air and land. Snakes, like all creatures that crawl, love the ground but avoid open air. Fish thrive in deep waters, and birds enjoy life in the skies. Those birds that fly highest find joy in the heat of the sun and remain close to it. Some creatures, like salamanders, even live within fire.

The elements surround and bind the body, and every soul in a body feels the weight of these elements. As a result, every soul is drawn to certain elements and repelled by others, which keeps it from finding perfect happiness. Yet, since the soul is divine, it continues to seek and reflect, even while trapped in a physical form. However, the soul's thoughts are not as free as they would be without the body. If the body is troubled by illness or fear, the soul is thrown into confusion, just as a man is tossed around by stormy waves.

PART 3

You have given me wonderful knowledge, powerful Mother Isis, about how God creates souls, and I am amazed by it. But you have not yet explained where souls go when they leave their bodies. I deeply wish to understand this mystery and will be grateful for your guidance. Isis replied: Listen carefully, my son, for this is a very important question, and it must not be overlooked. I will answer you fully. Do not think that when souls leave their bodies, they get lost in the vastness of the universe, merging into a boundless spirit with no way to return to a body or retain their identity. Imagine water spilled from a vase—it cannot return to the vase, and instead, it mixes with all other water. But this is not what happens with souls, wise Horos. I have been initiated into the mysteries of the immortal soul, and I walk the path of truth. I will tell you everything, leaving nothing out.

Water is made up of countless fluid particles without reason or purpose, while the soul is an individual being, created by God's mind and hands, filled with intelligence. Souls are born from unity, not from many things, so they do not mix with other beings. To join the soul with a body, God enforces a union through divine necessity. Souls do not return to the same place by chance or in confusion but are sent to the place that matches their experience. What they go through while living in a body, which weighs them down and limits them, determines where they will go next.

Listen to this example, my beloved Horos. Imagine a prison filled with people, eagles, doves, swans, hawks, swallows, sparrows, flies, serpents, lions, leopards, wolves, dogs, hares, oxen, sheep, and amphibious animals like seals, turtles, hydras, and crocodiles. Now imagine all these creatures being set free at the same time. Each would go where it belongs—humans to cities and public places, eagles to the sky, doves to the lower air, hawks to the higher air, swallows to places where people gather, sparrows to orchards, and swans to places where they can sing. Flies would stay close to the ground, living off the smells and vapors they find there. Lions and leopards would run to the mountains, wolves to remote places, dogs would follow humans, hares would go to the woods, oxen to fields, and sheep to pastures. Serpents would seek caves in the earth. Seals and turtles would return to shallow waters and rivers, living as they are meant to, close to both land and water. Every creature knows where it belongs, guided by

54

its nature. In the same way, every soul—whether it lived as a human or some other form—knows where it must go. It would be as foolish as saying a bull could live in water or a turtle could survive in the air to believe that souls would forget their place.

Even while they are trapped in flesh and blood, souls obey the laws of order, even though living in a body is a kind of punishment. How much more, then, will they follow these laws when they are free from the body! This sacred law applies to everything, even reaching up to the heavens. Now, my noble son, listen to how the hierarchy of souls is arranged. The space between the highest heaven, called the empyrean, and the moon is filled with gods, stars, and divine powers. Below the moon, between it and the earth, lies the home of souls.

The endless air, which we call wind, has its own paths to follow as it moves across the earth to give it life. But the movement of the wind does not block the path of souls. Souls travel freely through the air without mixing with it, much like water gliding over oil. This space between the earth and the heavens is divided into four main sections and sixty smaller regions. The first section starts from the earth and rises through four regions until it reaches certain high points, which it cannot go beyond.

The second province includes eight regions where the winds begin their movement. Pay close attention, my son, for you are hearing the hidden mysteries of the earth, the sky, and the sacred fluid that lies between them. Now, I will tell you, my glorious Horos, which souls inhabit each of these regions, starting with the highest. In the province of the winds, the birds fly, for beyond that point, there is no moving air, and no creatures can live there.

However, the air spreads into every corner within its reach and fills all the boundaries of the four directions of the earth, even though the earth itself cannot rise into the homes of the air.

The third province contains sixteen regions filled with a pure and delicate element. The fourth province has thirty-two regions where the air becomes so thin and clear that fire can pass through it without resistance. This is the order that rules from the lowest point to the highest: four main divisions, twelve intervals, and sixty regions, where each soul lives according to its nature. Though all souls share the same essence, they are arranged in a hierarchy. The farther a region is from the earth, the greater the dignity of the souls living there.

The space between the earth and the heavens is divided into these regions with careful order and harmony, my son Horos. Different people have called them by many names—zones, firmaments, or spheres. These are the places where souls dwell—both those who have been freed from their bodies and those who have not yet taken one. The position each soul occupies reflects its worth. Divine and royal souls reside in the upper regions, while the less noble souls remain close to the surface of the earth. Souls of ordinary rank inhabit the middle areas.

The souls destined to rule descend from the higher zones. When these souls are freed from their bodies, they return to their original home, or even to a higher realm—unless, of course, they have acted in ways that go against their dignity and God's laws. If they have failed, divine Providence sends them to lower regions according to their mistakes. Similarly, souls of lower rank may be moved to higher places as they grow in strength and honor.

Two great ministers serve universal Providence. One guards the souls, and the other leads them, giving them bodies and guiding them through their paths. The first minister protects the souls, while the second binds or releases them according to God's will. This sacred law of fairness governs the changes above, just as it shapes and forms the physical bodies in which the souls are housed.

This law works alongside two forces: Memory and Experience. Memory ensures that all things in creation retain their original design, as determined in the heavens. Experience ensures that every soul receives a body that matches its nature. Passionate souls are given strong bodies, lazy souls weak ones, active souls energetic bodies, gentle souls peaceful ones, powerful souls robust forms, and cunning souls are given quick and nimble bodies. In short, every soul is provided with the right kind of body.

There is wisdom in the way all creatures are formed. Birds are covered with feathers, intelligent beings are given sharp senses, and animals in the wild are equipped with horns, tusks, claws, or other defenses. Reptiles, with their smooth and flexible bodies, are also given sharp teeth or scales to protect them from harm, since their moist nature could otherwise make them weak. Fish, being timid creatures, are given a home in water, where the power of fire is dulled, for it can neither shine nor burn in that element.

Each fish swims freely using its fins, moving wherever it chooses, and its weakness is hidden by the darkness of the deep water. In the same way, souls are placed in bodies that suit their nature: rational souls in human bodies, wild souls in flying creatures, and souls without reason in beasts, whose only rule is strength.

Deceptive souls dwell in reptiles, for they do not attack openly but strike by hiding and waiting. Timid souls inhabit fish, as they are not fit to live in other elements. Yet in every kind of creature, there are some that act against their nature.

How does this happen, Mother? asked Horos. And Isis replied: A person might act without reason, a beast might escape the need for survival, a reptile may forget its cunning, a fish could lose its fear, and a bird might abandon its freedom. You have now heard about the hierarchy of souls, their descent, and how bodies are created. In each type of soul, there are some royal ones, with various qualities—some fiery, some cold, some proud, some gentle, some clever, some simple, some thoughtful, and others active. These differences reflect the regions from which the souls descend into bodies. Royal souls come from a royal realm, though there are many kinds of royalty—spiritual, physical, artistic, intellectual, and moral.

How do you describe these kinds of royalty? asked Horos. Isis answered: The king of souls is your father, Osiris. The king of bodies is the ruler of each nation. The king of wisdom is the Father of all things. The master of knowledge is Hermes Trismegistus, and Asclepius, the son of Hephaestus, presides over medicine. Power belongs to Osiris, and after him, to you, my son. Philosophy is guided by Arnebaskenis, and poetry by Asclepius, the son of Imhotep. So, as you reflect on this, you will see that there are many forms of kingship. The highest form of royalty belongs to the highest realm, while the lesser ones correspond to the different regions from which they originate. Souls born from the fiery realm handle fire; those from the watery realm thrive in water; those from the realms of art and knowledge pursue these paths;

and those from the realm of idleness live in ease. Everything that happens on earth has its origin in the higher realms, where all things are measured and balanced. Nothing begins here that does not first come from above and eventually return there.

Explain this further, Mother, said Horos. And Isis replied: Nature has stamped this truth into every creature. We breathe in air from above, exhale it, and breathe it in again through our lungs, which are made for this purpose. When our lungs can no longer receive air, we leave this life. Other disruptions can also break the balance of our nature.

What do you mean by this balance, Mother? Horos asked. Isis answered: It is the mixing and union of the four elements, which produce a vapor that surrounds the soul and enters the body, giving both a certain nature. This combination explains the variety in both souls and bodies. If fire is the dominant element in the body, the soul—already fiery—becomes even more energetic, and the body more lively and active. If air is dominant, both body and soul become unstable and restless. When water is the strongest element, the soul becomes gentle, kind, and adaptable, as water mixes easily with other things. If there is too much water, the body becomes soft and weak, easily broken by illness. If earth is dominant, the soul becomes slow, as the body's dense structure prevents clear expression. Such a soul turns inward, burdened by the heavy body, which moves slowly and with effort. But when all elements are balanced, the entire nature becomes lively in action, quick in movement, sensitive in perception, and strong in health.

Birds are born from a mixture of air and fire, matching the nature of the elements that form them. Humans have a large amount of fire, with a little air, and equal parts of water and earth. This abundance of fire gives humans intelligence, for thought is like a flame—it burns through obstacles, not with destruction, but by insight.

When water and earth dominate, with a little air and very little fire, animals are born. Those that have more fire than others are braver. When water and earth are present in equal amounts, reptiles are formed. Lacking fire, these creatures have no courage or honesty. Too much water makes them cold, while too much earth makes them dull and heavy, and with little air, they struggle to move easily. Creatures like fish are born when water far exceeds the amount of earth. Without fire or air, they are timid and prefer to stay hidden. The heavy presence of water and earth in their nature makes them similar to the way soil dissolves in water.

The growth of the body happens through the balanced increase of these elements. When the right amount is reached, growth stops. As long as the original balance of fire, air, earth, and water stays the same, the creature stays healthy. But if these elements lose their balance—whether by too much or too little fire, air, water, or earth—illness will arise. I am not talking about changes in activity or shifts in order, but rather a disruption in the balance itself. If air and fire, which are closest to the soul's nature, become too strong, the creature loses its natural state, as these elements tend to weaken the body.

The body relies on earth to sustain it, while water helps bind it together. Air provides movement, and fire gives energy. When these elements combine, they create vapors that merge with the soul, influencing it with their own qualities, whether good or bad. As long as the soul stays in harmony with these elements, it maintains its current state. But if the balance shifts, the relationship between the body and soul also changes. Fire and air, which naturally rise upward, pull the soul with them, while water and earth, which are drawn toward the ground, weigh down the body, making it heavy and keeping it tied to the earth.

• • •

A Treatise on Initiations; or, Asclepios

PART 1

Hermes: It is by the will of a god that you have come to us, Asclepios, so that you may take part in a divine discussion. This will be the most sacred teaching we have ever shared or been inspired to deliver. If you understand it, you will gain every blessing—though, perhaps, it is more accurate to say that all blessings are really just one, since they are all connected. They come from the same source, forming a unity that cannot be separated. You will understand this if you listen carefully to what we are about to say. But first, Asclepios, step away for a moment and find someone to join us for this discussion.

[Asclepios suggests inviting Ammon.]

There is no reason why Ammon cannot join us, replied Trismegistus. I have written to him before on topics about nature and other teachings, as I would to a beloved son. But it is your name, Asclepios, that I will place at the beginning of this work. Do not invite anyone else except for Ammon, for a conversation about the holiest matters should not be shared with too many. It would be wrong to reveal these divine teachings to a large audience, just as it would be wrong to share sacred truths with those who cannot understand or respect them.

[Ammon enters, completing the group, which now has four members.]

The presence of four is essential for these teachings, for they reflect the four great aspects of existence, representing the entirety of the universe. As Nebuchadnezzar said in the allegory recorded by Daniel, "The form of the fourth is like the Son of God." This shows how, through transformation instead of destruction, the earthly elements of man are purified by suffering.

Hermes: Every human soul, Asclepios, is immortal. But not every soul's immortality is the same. The way they experience it and the length of their journey differ from soul to soul.

Asclepios: That must be because not all souls are of the same kind, Trismegistus.

Hermes: You understand quickly, Asclepios! I haven't yet mentioned that everything is one, and one is everything. All things existed within the Creator before they came into being, and we call Him "all" because everything belongs to Him. Throughout this discussion, remember that the Creator is both One and All, the source of everything. All things flow from above—down to the earth, into the waters, and through the air. Fire alone rises, giving life, while everything that descends becomes subject to it.

What comes down from above creates, and what rises from below nourishes. The earth, which supports itself, receives and reshapes all that it takes in.

The universe contains everything and is everything. It moves the soul and the world and encompasses all that nature holds. Though life expresses itself in countless different forms, all these forms are connected, creating unity. Everything emerges from this oneness. The universe is made of four elements: fire, water, earth, and air. There is one world, one soul, and one God.

Now, focus your thoughts fully, for understanding the Divine requires divine help. This knowledge is like a powerful river rushing forward with great speed. It moves so quickly that it can easily escape the attention of those listening—and even the one who teaches it.

PART 2

Heaven, which reveals God, governs all things. The sun and moon determine the growth and decline of all bodies. But it is the true God—the Creator—who directs heaven, the soul, and everything that exists in the world. From His high place, countless influences flow down, spreading through the world into every soul, both in general and in specific ways, and into the nature of all things. God prepared the world to receive every individual form. Through Nature, He shapes these forms and draws the world upward toward heaven using the four elements. Everything follows God's plan, though the things that come from above are separated into individuals in a specific way.

Each type contains many individuals that share its nature. A type is whole, while each individual is a part of that whole. For example, gods make up one type, as do spirits, humans, birds, and all other beings in the world. These types create individual beings that resemble their original type. There is also a type without sensation but not without a soul—plants, which survive by rooting themselves in the earth. Individual plants can be found everywhere. Heaven is filled with God's presence. The types I mentioned extend all the way up to the beings whose individual souls are immortal. While types are eternal, not all individuals are. For example, humanity as a type is immortal, but individual humans are not.

Divine beings form a type where both the type and its individuals are as eternal as the divine itself. For other beings, only the type is eternal, while individual creatures die and are replaced through reproduction. Some individual beings are mortal. For example, man is mortal, but humanity as a whole is immortal. Yet, individual beings of all kinds can mix with those from other types. Some are original creations, while others are brought forth by gods, spirits, or humans. All of them resemble the type they come from. Bodies only take shape through divine will, individual beings take on their unique qualities with the help of spirits, and humans play a role in the care and training of animals.

Some spirits leave their original type and join with divine beings, becoming companions and allies of the gods. Those who keep their original character are called spirits and are drawn to things connected with humanity. Humans are similar to spirits, and in some ways, they even surpass them. Human individuality is complex and diverse because it results from the connections between different types. Humans serve as a vital link between many other kinds of beings. A person who aligns with the gods through intelligence and devotion becomes close to God. A person who aligns with spirits draws closer to them. Those who remain content with ordinary human life stay part of the human type. Other individuals will find themselves connected with the beings they are naturally drawn toward.

PART 3

Man, Asclepios, is a great wonder, a being worthy of admiration and respect. He moves within this divine world as though he were a god himself. He understands the nature of spirits and, knowing that he shares the same origin, he rises above his human side to focus on the divine within him. How fortunate and close to the gods mankind is! By connecting with the divine, man lets go of his earthly nature. Through love, he forms a bond with all other beings and feels his role is essential to the order of the universe. He looks toward the heavens and, from his place between the higher and lower realms, he loves everything beneath him and is loved by everything above him.

He works the land, harnesses the speed of the elements, and uses his sharp mind to explore the depths of the sea. Nothing is hidden from him. Heaven does not seem too distant, for knowledge lifts him up to it. His mind's brilliance is not dimmed by the thick air, the pull of the earth does not hold him back, and the depths of the ocean do not trouble him. He embraces everything and remains the same, no matter where he is.

All living beings seem to have roots that reach downward, but lifeless things have only one root that grows upward, supporting many branches like a tree. Some creatures live by feeding on two elements, while others need only one. There are also two kinds of nourishment—one for the soul and one for the body. The soul of the world is sustained by constant motion, while bodies grow through the nourishment provided by water and earth, the elements of the lower world. The spirit, which fills all things, mingles with everything and brings life to it. This spirit gives consciousness to intelligence, and through the fifth element—the ether—man receives the unique gift of awareness. In humans, this awareness becomes a deeper understanding of the divine order.

Since I am now speaking of consciousness, I will soon explain its purpose, which is as grand and sacred as divinity itself. But first, let us continue what we have already begun, speaking of humanity's union with the gods—a gift given only to mankind. Only a few people have the great fortune to understand the divine, a knowledge that exists only within God and the human mind.

Asclepios: Do all men have this awareness, Trismegistus?

Hermes: No, Asclepios, not everyone has true intelligence. Some people are deceived by the surface of things, following appearances without searching for their deeper meaning. This is where evil arises in man, causing the highest of creatures to lower himself to the level of animals. But I will explain more about consciousness and the mind later.

Man alone is made of two parts. One part is single and essential, as the Greeks say, formed in the image of the divine. The other part, which the Greeks call Kosmic, belongs to the material world and is made of four elements. This part makes up the body, which serves as a covering for the divine spirit within. The divine part, along with its pure perceptions and intelligence, hides behind the barrier of the physical body.

PART 4

Asclepios: Why, then, Trismegistus, was man placed in this world instead of with God, where he could live in perfect happiness?

Hermes: Your question is a reasonable one, Asclepios, and I ask God to help me answer it, for everything depends on His will— especially these great matters we are now discussing. Listen carefully, Asclepios. The Lord and Creator of all things, whom we call God, brought forth another God—one that can be seen and perceived by the senses. I call him sensible not because he possesses feelings, for this is not the place to discuss that, but because he is experienced through sight and touch. After bringing forth this being—who stands above all creatures and ranks second only to Himself—God saw that His creation was beautiful and filled with every kind of goodness. He loved it as His own child.

For God, to will something and to make it happen are one and the same. His will is instantly accomplished. Knowing that the essential part of man could not understand everything unless it was wrapped in the physical world, He gave man a body to dwell in. God wanted man to have two natures. He united and blended these natures perfectly. Through this, man could admire and worship the celestial and eternal things and also take care of and govern what is on earth.

Man was made with both spirit and body, with a nature that is partly eternal and partly mortal. This combination allows him to honor what is divine while managing the things of this world. I speak here of earthly things—not just the elements of earth and water that are under man's care, but also the things that come from him or depend on him. These include tending the land, raising livestock, building structures, creating ports, navigating the seas, engaging in trade, and carrying out exchanges that form the bonds between people.

Earth and water are part of the world, and this earthly part is supported by arts and sciences. Without these, the world would be incomplete in God's eyes. Whatever God wills must happen, and the result always accompanies His will. We cannot believe that anything which pleased Him at the beginning would stop pleasing Him, for from the very start He knew what would exist and what would bring Him joy.

PART 5

I see, Asclepios, that you are eager to understand how heaven and its inhabitants can become the focus of human aspiration and worship. Know then, Asclepios, that to seek after the God of heaven and all who dwell there is to offer them constant reverence, for man alone, among both divine and earthly beings, is capable of doing so. The admiration, worship, praise, and devotion of man bring joy to heaven and its celestial inhabitants. The Muses were sent to men by the supreme Divinity so that the earthly world would not lack the beauty of hymns, and so that the human voice might sing to the One who is All, the Father of everything. In this way, the gentle harmonies of earth are united with the choirs of heaven.

Only a few men, with minds pure and clear, are given the sacred task of seeing heaven clearly. Those whose minds are weighed down by the conflict between their earthly and divine natures are connected to the lower elements. Man is not lessened because he has a mortal part. In fact, his mortality increases his abilities and strength. His dual nature allows him to fulfill both earthly and divine roles. He is made in such a way that he can connect with both the physical world and the divine.

I hope, Asclepios, that you will give this teaching your full attention and focus, for many people lack faith in these things. Now I will explain the true principles for the benefit of the purest minds.

PART 6

The Master of Eternity is the first God, the world is the second, and man is the third. God, the Creator of the world and everything in it, governs the universe and places it under man's authority. In turn, man focuses his efforts on the world, making it his responsibility. The world and man are interconnected, each depending on the other, which is why the Greeks call the world Kosmos. Man understands both himself and the world, so he should know what aligns with his nature, what he can use, and what he should revere. As he offers praise and gratitude to God, he must also honor the world, which reflects God's image, just as man is also an image of God. God has two likenesses: the world and man.

Man's nature is complex. His soul, consciousness, mind, and reason are divine qualities, capable of reaching toward heaven. But his physical body, made of fire, water, earth, and air, is mortal and belongs to the earth, returning to it when life ends. In this way, man is made of both a divine part and a mortal part, with his body serving as the temporary vessel for the soul. The guiding principle of this dual nature is religion, and its result is goodness. Man reaches perfection when he frees himself from desires and rejects what is not truly part of him. The material things the body craves are external to the divine mind and can be called possessions only because they are not born with us but are acquired later. They are foreign to man's true nature, just as even the body itself is. For this reason, man must resist both the objects of desire and the part of him that makes him vulnerable to those desires.

It is man's duty to direct his soul through reason, allowing the contemplation of the divine to help him focus less on the mortal body that was given to him to care for the material world. For man to function fully, both his physical and spiritual aspects must work together. His body, with its two hands, two feet, and other organs, connects him to the lower, earthly world. At the same time, his inner nature is equipped with four essential faculties: sensibility, soul, memory, and foresight. These enable him to understand and perceive divine truths. With these abilities, man can explore differences, qualities, causes, and quantities. However, if the body weighs too heavily on him, it will prevent him from understanding the deeper truths of existence.

When man fulfills his purpose—governing the world and worshiping the Divine—what reward should he receive? If the world is the work of God, then the person who tends and enhances its beauty becomes a helper of God's will, using both his body and his daily efforts to serve what was created by God. What reward could be greater than the one given to our ancestors? May divine goodness grant us the same reward. All our hopes and prayers strive toward this goal: that we may be freed from the prison of the body and, released from the chains of mortality, return pure and sanctified to the divine inheritance of our nature.

Asclepios: What you say is just and true, Trismegistus. This is indeed the reward for honoring God and caring for the world. But those who live without piety are denied this return to the heavens. Instead, they must endure punishment, being sent into new bodies, a fate from which holy souls are spared.

The end of this teaching gives us the hope of an eternal future for the soul, a future earned through how we live in this world. Yet some find this idea hard to believe. To others, it is a mere story, and still others mock it. For many, the pleasures of the physical world are too sweet to resist. That is the problem—they become attached to their mortal part, forgetting their divine nature, and they lose sight of immortality.

I tell you this with prophetic insight: in the future, no one will choose the simple path of philosophy, which consists of studying divine things and practicing holy religion. Most people will complicate philosophy with all sorts of questions, adding subjects that do not belong to it. Why do they burden it with unnecessary sciences, and how do they mix it with so many irrelevant matters?

Hermes: Asclepios, they mix philosophy with all sorts of unnecessary subjects—like arithmetic, music, and geometry. But pure philosophy, which should focus on holy religion, should only touch on other sciences to admire the predictable movements of the stars, their positions, and their paths, as measured by calculation. It should explore the size of the earth, its qualities and quantities, the depths of the sea, and the power of fire. It should seek to understand the effects of these things and how Nature works, honoring both Art and the divine intelligence behind it. As for music, it is understood when one grasps reason and the divine order of the universe. This order arranges everything perfectly within the unity of the whole, creating a beautiful harmony and a divine melody.

Asclepios: What, then, will happen to men after us?

Hermes: Misled by the clever tricks of false teachers, they will stray from true, pure, and holy philosophy. To worship God with simple thoughts and a pure heart, to honor His works, and to bless His will—this alone is philosophy untouched by the distractions of idle curiosity. But that is enough on this subject.

PART 7

Let's begin by discussing Mind and related matters. In the beginning, there were God and Hylè—the Greek word for the first substance or matter of the universe. Spirit was present in the universe but not in the same way as with God. The things that make up the universe are not God; before they came into being, they did not exist, though they were contained in the source from which they would eventually emerge. Beyond created things is not only that which has yet to be born but also that which lacks the ability to create anything. Whatever has the power to create holds within it the seeds of all that can come into being, for it is natural that what exists can bring forth more existence.

God, however, is eternal and cannot be born. He always is, has been, and will be. His nature is to exist without a beginning. Matter, or the nature of the world, and mind both seem to have been brought forth at the beginning, possessing the ability to grow and create. The potential to generate life lies within Nature herself, and she acts as the source of creation without needing outside help. This is different from beings that can only create when they mix with something else. The universe holds within it all of Nature, acting as a womb for everything that exists. I call it a womb because nothing could come into being without a space to hold it. Everything that exists must occupy a place, for without a space to contain them, things could have no qualities, quantities, positions, or effects.

Although the world itself was not born, it holds within it the source of all creation, providing a fitting place for everything to be conceived. The universe contains the potential for both good and evil. This leads some to ask whether God could have prevented evil from existing. There is no need to answer them, but for you, Asclepios and Ammon, I will explain. Some say that God should have kept the world free from evil, but evil is an inherent part of creation. God has provided humanity with emotions, knowledge, and intelligence so that we can avoid evil. These gifts make humans superior to other animals, giving us the ability to recognize and escape evil before being trapped by it. True knowledge rests on supreme goodness.

Spirit animates and gives life to everything in the world. It acts as the tool through which the will of God is carried out. We must understand the supreme, invisible God through intelligence alone. This God directs the secondary, visible God—the universe—containing all space, matter, and energy, along with everything that can create and produce. Spirit, or Mind, governs all individual beings in the world according to the nature assigned to them by God. Matter—called Hylè or the Kosmos—serves as the container, motion, and reflection of everything that God directs. It provides each thing with what it needs and fills it with spirit according to its nature.

The universe takes the shape of a hollow sphere, containing within itself the reason for its form, though the cause of this form remains invisible. If someone were to examine any point on its surface and try to see what lies at its center, they would find nothing visible. The sphere can only be seen through the forms that appear on its surface, but in itself, it remains invisible. The center of this sphere—if it can be called a place—is known as Hades in Greek, meaning "the unseen," since it cannot be observed from the outside. The Greeks called the forms that shape reality "Ideas" because they represent the unseen patterns that give shape to everything. This hidden center, known as Hades by the Greeks, is called Hell (Inferno) by the Latins because of its deep and concealed location. These are the fundamental principles from which all things arise. Everything exists in them, through them, or emerges from them.

Asclepios: Are these principles the foundation of all individual beings, Trismegistus?

Hermes: Yes, the world sustains bodies, and spirit sustains souls. Thought, which is a gift from heaven and a privilege of humanity, nourishes intelligence, though only a few people have minds capable of receiving this gift. Thought is like a light that illuminates the mind, just as the sun illuminates the world. But it is even greater than the sun's light, which can be blocked by the moon or hidden when night falls. Once thought has entered the human soul, it becomes part of her nature and can never again be darkened by ignorance. This is why it is rightly said that the souls of the gods are pure intelligences. As for me, I say not this of all of them, but of the great supernal Gods.

PART 8

Asclepios: What are the fundamental principles of everything, Trismegistus?

Hermes: I am about to reveal to you profound and divine mysteries. As we begin, I ask for the favor of heaven, for these truths are not ordinary. There are many levels of divine beings, and each of them contains an element of intelligence. Do not think they are beyond our perception. In fact, we can understand them more clearly than things that are merely visible, as you will soon discover. If you pay close attention to what I am about to say, you will grasp this truth. These ideas are lofty and sacred, far beyond human understanding, so you must remain focused. If not, these words will pass through your mind without taking root, only to return to their source and be lost again.

There are gods above all visible forms, followed by spiritual gods. These gods, because they have both spiritual and physical

76

aspects, express their presence through their visible nature, with each one illuminating the others through their works. Everything is connected, from the center of creation to its farthest reaches, in accordance with the natural relationships between things. The supreme being of the heavens is called Zeus, for it is through the heavens that Zeus gives life to all things. The supreme being of the sun is light, which reaches us through the sun's disk. The thirty-six constellations are ruled by a being named Pantomorphos, meaning "one with all forms," because he gives divine shape to everything. The seven planets are governed by the spirits of Fortune and Destiny, who ensure the laws of Nature remain stable, even amid constant change. Ether serves as the medium through which everything is created.

Everything follows its kind: mortal beings are drawn to what is mortal, and visible things to what is visible. However, the ultimate guidance belongs to the highest master, so all diversity resolves back into unity. All things either emerge from unity or depend on it. Though things may appear separate, they are really parts of the same whole, which consists of two fundamental principles. These principles are the substance from which all things are made and the will of the One who shapes them.

Asclepios: What is the reason for this, Trismegistus?

Hermes: It is because God is the Father and ruler of everything. Though we may call Him by many names—each sacred in its own way—none of these names can fully describe His divine nature. Words are just sounds carried by air, expressing what a person's mind understands through the senses. Names, made of syllables and spoken aloud, are symbols that connect the voice to the ear.

But no matter how complex a name may be, it cannot capture the essence of the One who is the source of all greatness. Yet, since He must be named, we must either call Him "All" or refer to Him by the names of everything that exists.

He is both one and all, containing the fullness of both masculine and feminine principles. Through His own will, He continuously creates everything He intends. His will is universal goodness, and this same goodness is present in everything. Nature is born from His divine essence, ensuring that all things are exactly as they should be and that Nature itself has the power to give birth to everything that will come into existence.

This, Asclepios, is why everything has both male and female aspects.

Asclepios: Do you say this is true even of God, Trismegistus?

Hermes: Yes, not just of God but of all things, whether they are alive or not. Nothing that exists can be without the ability to create. If things could not bring forth life, they could not remain as they are. This law of creation is present in Nature, in the mind, and throughout the universe, sustaining everything that is brought into existence. Both male and female are full of creative power, and their union—or rather, their perfect merging—can be known as Eros, or Aphrodite, or even by both names together.

If the mind can grasp one truth more clearly than any other, it is this: the duty to create life is a law that the God of Nature has placed on all beings. To this law, He has also attached the highest joy, delight, longing, and the purest love. There would be no need to explain the importance of this law, since everyone can sense it within themselves. Notice how, at the moment when the essence of life flows from the brain, the two natures blend into each other. One eagerly draws in and hides the seed of the other. Through this joining, the female receives the strength of the male, and the male rests on the embrace of the female.

This sacred union is performed in secret, for if it were openly displayed, the divine nature of both would risk being mocked by those who do not understand. True piety is rare in this world, and it would not take long to count the few who possess it. Most people are filled with malice because they lack wisdom and knowledge of how the universe works. Understanding divine religion is the foundation of all things, leading to the rejection of vices and providing the remedy for them. But when ignorance takes hold, vice grows and wounds the soul in ways that are difficult to heal. A soul poisoned by vice swells with sickness, and only knowledge and understanding can restore it.

Let us continue this teaching, even if only a few will benefit from it. Now, Asclepios, listen carefully as I explain why God gave part of His intelligence and knowledge to humanity alone.

God the Father, the Ruler above all gods, gave man reason and intelligence to help him avoid or overcome the weaknesses of the body and to hold on to the hope of immortality. Man was created good, capable of living forever, and formed from two natures: one divine and one mortal. This dual nature makes man superior to both the gods, who possess only immortality, and mortal beings, who lack divinity. Because of this, man is closely connected to the gods, honoring them with religious devotion, and the gods, in turn, care for human affairs with affection. But I speak only of pious men. As for the wicked, I will not mention them here, for discussing them would spoil the holiness of this teaching.

PART 9

And since we are now speaking of the connection and similarity between humans and gods, consider the power and ability of man, Asclepios. Just as the Ruler and Father—whom we call God— created the celestial gods, man creates the gods that dwell in temples. These gods enjoy being close to humans, for they not only receive light but also give it in return. This connection benefits both mankind and the gods, strengthening them.

Does this surprise you, Asclepios? Do you doubt it, as many others do?

Asclepios: I am amazed, Trismegistus, but I accept your words. I see that man is truly fortunate to have such a gift.

Hermes: Yes, he is indeed worthy of admiration, for he is the greatest of all gods. The celestial gods are made from the purest part of Nature, without any mixture of other elements, and their visible forms are like heads only.

Asclepios: But the gods made by humans have two aspects— one divine, which is their purest nature, and the other human, formed from earthly matter. These gods not only have heads but also full bodies, with all their limbs. This means that humans, remembering their own nature and origins, imitate the divine by creating these gods. Just as the Father and Lord shaped the eternal gods to reflect Himself, so mankind creates gods in its own image. Are you referring to statues, Trismegistus?

Hermes: Yes, I am speaking of statues, Asclepios. How little faith you have! What else could I mean but these statues, which are so full of life, emotion, and purpose? They perform many amazing acts—some offer prophecies by sending dreams or other signs, while others bring illness or healing according to what people deserve.

Do you not understand, Asclepios, that Egypt is a reflection of heaven, a mirror of the divine order on earth? In truth, this land is the temple of the world. Yet, as wise men must foresee what is to come, there is something you should know. A time will come when it will seem that all the Egyptians' devotion to the gods was for nothing and that their prayers have gone unanswered. The divine presence will leave the earth and return to the heavens, abandoning Egypt, which was once its sacred home. Religion will fade, and the gods will no longer be found here. Foreigners will overrun the land, and not only will sacred practices be neglected, but religion, worship, and reverence for the gods will be outlawed and punished by law.

The land, once filled with temples, will become full of tombs and the dead. O Egypt, Egypt, all that will remain of your religion will be legends that future generations will not believe. Only the words carved into stone will bear witness to your devotion. Barbarians—whether from Scythia, India, or other neighboring lands—will take control of Egypt. The gods will return to the heavens, and mankind, abandoned, will be lost. Egypt will be left empty, deserted by both men and gods.

I call upon you, O sacred River, to bear witness to what is to come! Waves of blood will stain your waters, overflowing your banks. The dead will outnumber the living, and if any Egyptians survive, they will no longer act as Egyptians but as foreigners in their own land.

You weep, Asclepios, but even sadder things will come to pass. Egypt will fall into apostasy, the worst of all evils. Once the sacred land loved by the gods, Egypt will become a place of corruption, a school of impiety, and a home to all forms of violence. People will grow tired of everything. They will no longer admire or love the world. They will turn away from this beautiful creation, which is the most perfect work of all time—past, present, and future. The weariness of their souls will leave them with nothing but contempt for the universe, this magnificent creation of God. They will reject this masterpiece, in which God's will united everything in perfect harmony, worthy of eternal reverence, praise, and love.

Darkness will be preferred to light, and death will seem better than life. No one will look toward heaven. Those who remain faithful to religion will be seen as fools, while the wicked will be praised as wise. The violent will be honored as heroes, and the evil-hearted will be celebrated as the best of men. Everything related to the soul—whether mortal or capable of eternal life— will be mocked and dismissed as foolishness. Faithful people will even face death for their beliefs. Believe me, Asclepios, those who remain true to religion and wisdom will face great danger.

New laws and customs will arise, and not a single sacred word or belief will remain—nothing religious or worthy of heaven will endure. What a tragic separation there will be between gods and humans! Evil spirits will be all that remain, and they will mix with the suffering human race, driving people toward wickedness, war, greed, lies, and everything that goes against the nature of the soul. The earth will lose its balance, the seas will become impossible to navigate, and even the stars will stray from their usual paths. Every holy voice will be silenced, crops will rot, and the land will no longer be fruitful. Even the air will become heavy with gloom. This will be the world's old age, a time marked by irreligion, disorder, lawlessness, and the confusion of good people.

When all of these things come to pass, Asclepios, the Lord and Father—sovereign God over all the world—will see the evil ways and actions of men. Then, through His divine will and goodness, He will put an end to these misfortunes. To stop the errors and corruption, He may flood the world, burn it with fire, or destroy it with wars and plagues. Afterward, He will restore the world to its original beauty, making it once more a place worthy of admiration and worship. Songs of praise and blessing will again celebrate Him, the One who created and redeemed this marvelous work.

This rebirth of the world, the restoration of all good things, and the renewal of Nature will happen at the appointed time, according to the eternal and unchanging will of God.

Asclepios: Truly, Trismegistus, God's nature reflects His will, which is absolute goodness and wisdom.

Hermes: Yes, Asclepios, will arises from reflection, and to will is itself an act of choice. God, who contains everything and has everything He desires, wills nothing out of whim. Everything He wills is good, and He possesses all that He wills. Whatever is good, He thinks and wills, for such is His nature. The world reflects His righteousness.

Asclepios: Then the world is good, Trismegistus?

Hermes: Yes, Asclepios, the world is good, as I will now explain. Just as God grants all beings various gifts—such as thought, soul, and life—the world distributes good things to mortals. These include the changing seasons, the fruits of the earth, birth, growth, maturity, and other blessings.

Though God is beyond the highest heavens, He is also present everywhere, watching over all things. Beyond the heavens lies a starless sphere, which surpasses all physical existence. Between the heavens and the earth rules the giver of life, whom we call Zeus (Jupiter). Over the earth and sea reigns the one who nourishes all living creatures, as well as the plants and fruit-bearing trees—this is Zeus Sarapis (Jupiter Plutonius).

Those who are destined to rule the earth will be sent to the farthest reaches of Egypt, to a city built toward the west, where people from every part of the world will gather by land and sea.

Asclepios: And where are they now, Trismegistus?

Hermes: They are already established in a great city on the mountain of Libya. But enough of this.

PART 10

Let us now discuss what is mortal and what is immortal. People who do not understand the nature of things are troubled by the thought and fear of death. Death happens when the body, exhausted by its work, falls apart. When the force that holds the body together reaches its limit, the body can no longer carry the burdens of life, and so it dies. Death is simply the breaking down of the body and the end of physical sensations. There is no need to trouble ourselves over it. However, there is another law that people often ignore or refuse to believe.

Asclepios: What is this law that people overlook?

Hermes: Listen carefully, Asclepios. When the soul leaves the body, it comes under the power of God, who judges it according to its deeds. If the soul is found to be pious and just, it is allowed to dwell in the divine realms. But if it is stained with vice, it is cast down, tossed between the forces of air, fire, and water. Such a soul is caught in endless storms, drifting between heaven and earth, condemned to eternal punishment. Its immortality only ensures that it suffers the consequences of its actions without end.

We should fear such a terrible fate. Those who now doubt the truth of these things will be forced to believe—not through words, but by the suffering they will endure.

Asclepios: So human laws alone are not enough to punish wrongdoing?

Hermes: Everything on earth is mortal, Asclepios. Those who live according to the desires of the body, without obeying the laws that guide human life, face even greater punishment after death. The punishment will be especially harsh for those whose sins were hidden, for God knows everything and ensures the punishment fits the crime.

Asclepios: Who suffers the greatest punishment, Trismegistus?

Hermes: Those who die violent deaths for their crimes seem to escape the debt they owe to Nature. Their earthly punishment might appear to be the result of their actions, but they still owe a debt. Because they could not pay this debt while alive, they must suffer greatly after death. Without the chance to correct their actions or seek forgiveness, they are delivered into torment until their debt is fully paid.

The Father and Lord of all things, who is everything and rules over all, reveals Himself willingly to everyone. However, He does not show His dwelling place, His glory, or His greatness. Instead, He grants people understanding through intelligence, which clears away ignorance and reveals the truth.

A just person finds strength in religion and piety, and God protects him from harm. Through this connection with divine intelligence, man rises above his mortal nature and hopes for eternal life. This is the difference between the good and the wicked. The person who is guided by piety, wisdom, and devotion to God gains true understanding, as if seeing with open eyes. This faith gives him confidence and allows him to rise above others, just as the sun shines brighter than the other lights in the sky.

If the sun gives light to the other stars, it is not only because of its size and strength, but because of its divine nature and holiness. You must see the sun, Asclepios, as a secondary god that governs the rest of the world, giving light to everything, both living and non-living. If the world is a living being—one that exists, has always existed, and will always exist—then nothing within it is truly mortal. Every part of it is alive, for in something that lives forever, death has no place. In the same way, God is the fullness of life and eternity, for He must live forever. The sun, which endures as long as the universe, continuously sustains all living beings, acting as the source and provider of life.

God is the eternal ruler of everything that both gives life and receives it. He is the one who gave life to all living creatures through an unchanging law, which I will explain to you. The movement of the universe is what makes eternity alive, and the endless motion of life is what keeps the universe eternal. The universe will never stop moving, nor will it ever decay. Eternal life surrounds and protects it like a fortress, giving life to everything inside it and keeping everything connected under the sun's rule.

This movement has two effects: the universe is kept alive by the eternity that encircles it, and in turn, it gives life to all that it holds. This life spreads through everything, following specific patterns, numbers, and seasons. All things follow their appointed times according to the sun and the stars, under divine law. Earthly cycles are marked by changes in the atmosphere, through the shifts between heat and cold. Celestial cycles are measured by the movement of the stars, which return to the same places in the sky at regular intervals.

The universe is the stage on which time plays out, and its constant motion sustains life. Time and order ensure the renewal of all things through the recurring seasons.

PART 11

Since the universe is as it is, nothing in nature—whether in the heavens or on the earth—remains unchanged or stable. Only God is complete, perfect, and unchanging in Himself. He is firm in His stability and cannot be moved by anything, for everything exists within Him, and He alone is everything. If we say that God moves, it can only be within eternity. Yet eternity itself does not move, because time, with all its motion, exists within eternity and draws its meaning from it.

God has always been and will always remain unchanging. Together with God exists eternal stability, containing within it an unmanifest universe—an image of the eternal world that has yet to appear. The created universe mirrors this eternal one. Time, though constantly moving, has its own kind of stability because it repeats its cycles endlessly. So, while eternity is fixed and unchanging, time flows within it, and this flow is essential to the nature of time. It may seem as though eternity moves because of the motion within time, and in the same way, it might seem that God Himself moves within His unchanging nature.

Even in the vast balance of existence, there is a kind of movement within what does not change. The law of God's immensity remains unaltered. The Infinite, the Unknowable, and the Immeasurable cannot be grasped or carried by anything. We cannot know where it comes from, where it is going, where it exists, or what it truly is. It rests within its own perfect stability, just as its stability rests within it. Whether God exists within eternity or eternity exists within God—or both exist within each other—remains a mystery beyond understanding.

Eternity cannot be measured by time, and time—defined by cycles, numbers, and repeating patterns—shares in eternity. Both time and eternity appear endless. Stability, as the foundation of all movement, holds the highest place because everything relies on stability. Thus, God and eternity are the source of all things, while the changing world cannot be considered their source. The changing nature of the world outweighs its stability, following the law of eternal movement within balance.

The divine consciousness is unchanging, moving only within perfect equilibrium. It is holy, incorruptible, and eternal. Or, to say it more clearly, it is the essence of eternity itself— rooted in the absolute truth of the Supreme God, filled with all understanding and knowledge, or, simply put, in God Himself. The consciousness of the natural world includes everything that can be sensed, while human consciousness holds memory, which allows us to recall what we have done. The divine consciousness reaches even to human beings, though God did not extend this supreme awareness to all creatures, for if every living thing shared it, the divine glory would be lessened.

The intelligence of the human mind depends entirely on memory, and it is through memory that humans have become masters of the earth. The intelligence of nature and the essence of the universe can be understood through the things we can see and experience. Eternity reveals its nature through the physical world.

However, the consciousness of the Divine Being, the awareness of the Supreme God, is the only true reality. This truth cannot be found—even as a shadow—within the ever-changing world, which is full of illusions, shifting appearances, and errors. In this world, everything is understood only in terms of time.

Do you see, Asclepios, how profound these matters are? I thank the Most High God for granting me the light of His grace. And to you, Tat, Asclepios, and Ammon, I say: keep these divine mysteries within your hearts, and speak of them only in silence.

There is a difference between perception and intellect. The intellect, through study, can understand the nature of the universe. The universal mind connects to the awareness of eternity and the divine beings beyond this world. Yet, as humans, we can only glimpse these heavenly things as if through a mist, because the limits of our senses allow us to see them only dimly. Our strength is too small to fully grasp such divine truths, but when we do manage to reach them, we are blessed with the joy of knowing them deep within ourselves.

PART 12

Regarding the concept of the void, to which many people give great importance, I believe it does not exist, has never existed, and never will. Every part of the universe is filled, just as the earth is full of bodies of different shapes and qualities. Some bodies are larger, others smaller; some are solid, others light or thin. The larger, more solid things are easy to see, while the smaller, more delicate ones are harder to notice or even invisible.

We can only recognize them through touch. Many people believe these things are not real bodies but just empty spaces. However, true emptiness cannot exist.

If there were something beyond the universe—though I do not believe this—it would still be filled with divine beings suited to the nature of such a place. The world we see is filled with bodies appropriate to its qualities. We do not perceive everything within the world. Some things are vast, others small. Some seem tiny only because they are far away, or our vision is too weak to notice them. Other things may be so fine and subtle that we are entirely unaware of them. I am referring to the spirits and heroes that dwell between us and the higher skies, where there are no clouds or storms.

It is incorrect to say that any space is truly empty unless we specify what it is empty of—whether fire, water, or something else. Even if a space lacks one of these elements, it is never without spirit or air. The same is true of the idea of "place." A place only makes sense when it refers to something within it. Saying "place" without naming what belongs there makes no sense. For example, we say "the place of water" or "the place of fire." Just as there can be no space completely empty of everything, there is no such thing as place on its own. If a place were entirely empty, it would not exist. For this reason, in my view, no such empty place exists within the universe.

If nothing is truly empty, then space cannot exist on its own unless it has dimensions like length, width, and depth, just as human bodies have their own defining characteristics. If this is true, then we must understand that the higher world—what we call God, who is only known through intelligence—is incorporeal. Nothing material can mix with His nature or be described by qualities, quantities, or measurements. None of these things belong to Him.

This world that we call the physical world holds all things that can be seen, touched, or measured. But even this universe cannot exist without God. God is everything, and everything comes from Him and depends on His will. He contains all that is good, orderly, wise, and perfect. Only He can fully know and understand these things. Nothing exists without Him. Everything that was, is, or will be originates from Him, is contained within Him, and relies on Him—whether it be qualities, sizes, or countless forms.

If you understand this, Asclepios, give thanks to God. When you observe the universe, recognize that everything in this world, with all it contains, is wrapped like a garment by the higher, divine world. All beings—whether mortal or immortal, rational or irrational, living or non-living—carry the nature of the class to which they belong. Although each creature shares the general characteristics of its kind, there are also differences within every kind. Humanity, too, has a common type, though individual people differ from one another.

The essence that comes from God is without a body, as is everything that belongs to intelligence. Since there are two sources of form—one material and the other immaterial—it is impossible for anything created to be an exact copy of something else, no matter how much time or space separates them. Forms are constantly changing, just like the passing moments of an hour. Yet the world, which moves in endless cycles, reflects the nature of God, who contains all forms within Himself. Each form continues to exist, creating countless versions of itself as time moves forward. The world changes as it revolves, but the essence of each kind remains the same. While individual forms within a species may vary, the essence of the species does not change.

Asclepios: Does the world also change in its form, Trismegistus?

Hermes: Asclepios, have you not been paying attention? The world consists of everything that is created within it. Are you asking about the heavens, the earth, and the elements? These things also change in their appearance. The sky, for example, is sometimes rainy, sometimes dry; sometimes hot, sometimes cold. It may be bright or covered with clouds. Though it seems to remain the same, it constantly shifts.

The earth, too, changes. At times, it brings forth fruit, and at other times, it hides it away. It produces many different kinds of plants, trees, flowers, and seeds, each with unique properties, colors, scents, and shapes. Fire also transforms in many ways. The sun and moon show us different phases and appearances, like the reflections we see in mirrors.

We have now said enough on these matters.

PART 13

Let us turn our attention back to people and explore the gift of reason, which gives humans the right to be called rational beings. Among all the amazing things about humanity, one stands out the most: humans have discovered the divine force within nature and learned how to use it for their purposes. Long ago, our ancestors, confused about their beliefs in the gods and unable to reach an understanding of divine truth and religion, developed the art of making gods. Once they learned this art, they gave their creations special powers taken from the natural world. But since they couldn't create souls, they called on the spirits of beings like angels and genii to fill their sacred images and ceremonies with life. This gave these idols the ability to bring about good or bad outcomes.

In this way, Asclepios, the founder of medicine, has a temple on a mountain in Libya, near a river known for its crocodiles. There, his earthly body rests. As for his spirit—the better part of him—it resides elsewhere. The idea behind this is explored further in earlier sections. Understanding these thoughts requires some knowledge of occult teachings, especially about spirits connected to the world and nature. In ancient times, people believed that the idols representing their gods had powers, just as many today believe that certain statues of saints have special abilities. For example, we hear stories of how a particular statue of the Virgin Mary in one town grants prayers, while another in a different place does not. Even now, sacred images are said to heal the sick, stop plagues, uncover hidden water sources, and bless worshippers.

Hermes explains that these abilities come from the divine power in nature, which humans shape to suit their needs. Humanity, he argues, must first go through the stage of worshipping nature before it can fully understand the divine order and recognize the existence of heavenly gods. Before human intelligence can reach the highest spiritual realms, it must pass through the levels between earth and heaven. This is why people first worship the images of gods before they come to know the gods themselves.

These images are not always made of wood or stone. In fact, every personality is like an idol, reflecting deeper truths and holding a part of the divine essence. Though these images seem powerful and worthy of worship to those who don't understand true divine religion, Hermetists see them as symbols of essential truths that exist beyond any physical form and remain unchanged by it.

There are three signs of true divinity: it goes beyond physical form, beyond time, and beyond individual personalities. Instead of physical form, there is pure essence. Instead of time, there is eternity. Instead of individual people, there are universal principles. Events turn into continuous processes, and what we think of as physical occurrences become inner realities.

As long as any idea of the divine is tied to a physical event or historical fact, it shows that the heavenly realm has not been reached. Symbols, once recognized as symbols, are no longer misleading or harmful. They act like veils of light, revealing glimpses of the "Divine Darkness," which is the ultimate goal of the true Hermetist. Even the most refined or abstract way of expressing supreme truth is still only a symbol or metaphor. The real truth is something beyond words, only known from God to God. It is pure essence, silence, and darkness.

The person who understands this truth—because consciousness and life are one with the whole person—returns to the divine realm. Through his divinity, he offers help to the sick, just as he once taught people the art of healing. Likewise, Hermes, my ancestor whose name I carry, now rests in the land named after him. People from all over come to his shrine to seek health and guidance through their prayers. We also see how Isis, the wife of Osiris, brings blessings to people when she is pleased, and misfortune when she is angry. These earthly gods can feel both kindness and anger, as they are shaped from nature by humans. This explains why in Egypt, people worship animals, and cities honor the souls of those who gave them laws and whose names they still remember. For this reason, Asclepios, gods worshipped in one place might be ignored elsewhere, which often causes conflicts between cities in Egypt.

Asclepios: What kind of divinity do these earthly gods possess, O Trismegistus?

Hermes: Their divinity lies in the spiritual essence found in plants, stones, and fragrant substances. This is why these gods are drawn to sacrifices, songs of praise, and sweet music that echoes the harmony of the heavens. These rituals attract them to their shrines, where they remain among humans for long periods. This is how people create gods. But do not think, Asclepios, that the actions of these earthly gods are random. While the gods in the heavens maintain their order and position above, these earthly gods also have their own roles. Some predict the future through signs and divination, while others assist with different aspects of life, acting as helpers, family, or friends to those who call upon them.

PART 14

Asclepios: O Trismegistos, what role does Destiny or Fate play in how things work? If the heavenly gods rule the universe and the earthly gods control specific events, where does Destiny fit in?

Hermes: O Asclepios, Destiny is the force that makes everything happen. It's like a chain connecting all events together. It's the reason behind everything and can be seen as the highest power—or rather, the second god, created by God Himself. It's the law governing everything in both heaven and earth, based on divine rules. Destiny and Necessity are inseparable: Destiny starts everything, and Necessity makes sure things unfold as they were meant to. From this process, Order arises—it's the way things follow one another in Time, for nothing can happen without Order. This is how the world becomes complete. The world is built on Order, and the universe holds together because of it.

These three forces—Destiny (or Fate), Necessity, and Order—completely depend on God's will. He governs the world through divine reason and law. These forces have no will of their own; they are unmoved by anger or kindness. They are simply the tools of eternal Reason, which never changes, never wavers, and never breaks.

Destiny comes first, carrying within it the seeds of future events, just like freshly planted soil contains seeds waiting to grow. Next is Necessity, which pushes these events to happen. Lastly, Order keeps everything in place, ensuring that what Destiny and Necessity create holds together. This entire process is a never-ending cycle, with no clear beginning or end. It continues forever, governed by an unchanging law that flows through eternity. As time moves on, things that once disappeared rise again, and what was on top sinks back down. This is how the circular movement works. Everything is so connected that it's impossible to tell where one thing begins or ends. They follow and lead each other endlessly.

However, chance and luck still influence earthly events.

PART 15

Now that we have spoken of all things within our reach, as much as God has allowed, it is time to offer our blessings and prayers to Him and return to our earthly responsibilities. After filling our minds with sacred knowledge, which nourishes the soul, we leave the sanctuary and lift our prayers to God. Turning toward the south, they began their orations, for it is proper to look toward the sun's descent when offering praise, just as one should face the east at sunrise to honor the new day. While they prayed, Asclepios spoke quietly: "O Tatius, let us ask our Father to allow our prayers to rise with the fragrance of incense and perfumes."

Trismegistos overheard him and responded with emotion: "May the omen be favorable, O Asclepios. But to burn incense or perfume during prayer is almost a sacrilege. He who is all things and contains all things needs nothing from us. We should offer Him only our praise and devotion. The purest offering is the grace we give in worship."

They prayed: "We thank You, O Most High, for through Your grace, we have received the light of knowledge. May Your name be praised and honored, for it is the name through which divinity is worshipped in the tradition of our ancestors! You grant us the gifts of faith, love, and devotion, and above all, You bless us with awareness, reason, and understanding. Through awareness, we recognize You; through reason, we seek You; and through understanding, we rejoice in knowing You.

"By Your divine power, we are saved, and we take joy in seeing Your presence revealed. We are grateful that from the time we came into this body, You have chosen to prepare us for eternity. Our only true joy is the knowledge of Your greatness. We have come to know You, O magnificent Light, grasped only through understanding. We have known You, O true Path of Life, inexhaustible Source of all creation! We have known You, O abundant Spirit of Nature, unchanging and eternal!

"In this prayer, we honor Your holy sanctity and ask only that You allow us to continue loving Your truth, so we may never stray from this way of life. Filled with this hope, we now go forth to enjoy a pure meal, free from the flesh of animals."

• • •

The Definitions of Asclepios

PART 1

Asclepios to the King Ammon. I send you, O King, an important message. I will begin by calling upon God, the Master of the Universe, the Creator and Father of everything. He contains all things, is everything in one, and is one in everything. Everything that exists comes from unity and remains in unity. These two are not separate, for they are one. Keep this in mind, O King, throughout my entire message. It is pointless to try and separate the All from the One by calling everything "the All" and ignoring their unity. This distinction cannot be made because the All cannot exist without unity, just as unity cannot exist without the All. Unity always exists and never stops being one; otherwise, all things would fall apart.

What I am saying goes against common beliefs and may even seem different from some of my other teachings. My teacher Hermes often spoke with me, either alone or with Tatios present. He used to say that those who read my writings would think they are simple and clear, but in truth, they contain deeper, hidden meanings. This hidden meaning has become harder to understand because the Greeks translated our words into their language, which caused misunderstandings. The Egyptian language has a special power that makes the meaning clear to the mind. As much as you can, O King—and you have great power—do not allow this message to be translated, or these mysteries may fall into Greek hands. Their polished way of speaking could weaken the seriousness and strength of these teachings. The Greeks love new ways of talking and are very wordy in their philosophy, while we focus more on actions and facts rather than many words.

In the earth, there are powerful springs of water and fire. These represent the three elements—fire, water, and earth—which all come from the same source. It shows that all matter comes from one great origin, filled with abundance, receiving its existence from above. This is how the Creator, through the sun, governs heaven and earth. The sun sends down essence and draws up matter, holding the universe together and giving everything life through its light. The sun spreads its energy not only in the heavens and air but also on earth and deep into the abyss. If there is an essence beyond what we can see, it must belong to the sun, and light is its messenger. Only the sun knows its true nature and origin.

To fully understand these hidden things, we would need to be close to the sun and share its nature. However, what the sun reveals to us is not guesswork—it is the brilliant vision that lights up both the heavens and the world. The sun stands at the center of the universe like a crown-bearer, guiding the world like a skilled charioteer. It controls the reins of life, soul, spirit, immortality, and birth, carrying everything along with it. Through this process, the sun forms everything and grants immortality to eternal beings.

The light that radiates outward nourishes the eternal spaces of the universe. The light that spreads across the waters, earth, and air becomes a fertile place where life begins. Here, all kinds of births and transformations take place, as things change from one form to another in a continuous spiral movement. This transformation allows creatures to move through different parts of the world, shifting between forms and appearances while keeping the balance of all these changes, just like in the creation of larger beings. The stability of physical forms comes from constant change, but immortal forms never break down, while mortal bodies do. This is the difference between what is immortal and what is mortal.

The sun creates life as constantly as it shines, without ever stopping. Surrounding it are countless groups of spiritual beings. These spirits stay close to the immortal gods and watch over human affairs. They carry out the will of the gods through storms, fires, earthquakes, wars, and famines to punish those who act against the divine. The greatest sin people can commit is disrespecting the gods. The gods are meant to do good, humans are meant to honor them, and the spirits are there to discipline those who stray.

The gods do not hold people accountable for mistakes made by accident, bold actions taken because of fate, or through ignorance. Only true wrongdoing falls under their judgment. The sun supports and sustains all living things, just as the Ideal World surrounds the physical world and fills it with countless forms. Similarly, the sun wraps everything in its light, bringing life and helping all creatures grow. When they become tired and weak, the sun gathers them back to itself. The sun commands the Genii—actually, many groups of Genii—whose numbers match the stars.

Every star has its own Genii, some naturally good, some bad, and others mixed, depending on what they do. A Genie's actions define its essence.

Some Genii perform both good and harmful deeds. All of these Genii oversee what happens on Earth. They disrupt governments and individual lives, shaping our souls. They are present in our nerves, marrow, veins, arteries, and even our brains and internal organs. When a person is born, they are assigned to Genii responsible for overseeing births, who operate under the influence of the stars. These Genii are constantly changing, moving in cycles, never staying the same. They act through the body to affect two parts of the soul, leaving their unique influence on each. However, the rational part of the soul is beyond the reach of the Genii, as it is meant to receive God's light, which shines like a ray from the sun.

Only a few people receive this divine light, and for those who do, the Genii have no power over them. Neither gods nor Genii can interfere when even a single ray from God touches someone. For all other people, both their souls and bodies are guided by Genii, and they become connected to these spiritual forces, mirroring their actions. Desire, which often misleads, is not the same as reason, which remains steady. The Genii control earthly matters and use our bodies as their tools. This influence is what Hermes refers to as Destiny.

The Intelligible World is linked to God, while the physical world is connected to the Intelligible World. Through these two realms, the sun transmits God's energy, which is creative in nature. Surrounding the sun are eight spheres: the sphere of the fixed stars, the six planetary spheres, and the sphere that encircles the Earth. The Genii are tied to these spheres, and humans are connected to the Genii, creating a chain that binds all beings to God, the universal Father. The sun is the source of creation, and the world is like a crucible where creation takes shape. The Intelligible Essence governs the heavens, the heavens guide the gods, the gods oversee the Genii, and the Genii direct human beings. This is the divine order, and through this hierarchy, God works through both gods and Genii to carry out His will.

Since everything is a part of God, God is present in all things. By creating everything, God is continually extending Himself without pause. God's energy exists only in the present, for it has no past, and because God has no limits, His creation has neither a beginning nor an end.

PART 2

If you think about it, O King, you'll realize that some things are both physical and non-physical. "Which things are those?" asked the King. Things like the images you see in mirrors—aren't they non-physical, even though they appear to be real? "That's true, Tat," the King replied. "You have quite an interesting way of thinking!" There are other non-physical things too, such as abstract ideas. Wouldn't you agree that these ideas are not physical themselves, but they still appear through living and non-living things? "That's true again, Tat," said the King. So, it seems that non-physical things reflect onto physical things, and physical things reflect back onto the non-physical. In other words, the physical world and the world of ideas mirror each other. Therefore, O King, honor the sacred images, for they are reflections of the physical world. The King then stood up and said, "I think it's time to take care of our guests, prophet. We can continue this theological discussion tomorrow."

PART 3

When a musician tries to play a melody but can't get the instruments to work together in harmony, his efforts end in failure, and the audience laughs. No matter how skilled he is or how hard he tries, he cannot blame the instrument for his inability to create music. The great musician of Nature, the God who oversees all harmony and controls how every instrument plays in perfect rhythm, never tires. Fatigue doesn't touch the gods. If a conductor leads a concert with trumpeters playing their parts, flute players performing the soft melodies, and lyres and violins accompanying the song, no one would blame the composer if one instrument plays out of tune. Instead, we honor the composer's talent, even if the music is disturbed by a single instrument.

In the same way, it would be disrespectful to blame Humanity for the failures of our physical bodies. God, the untiring Artist, is always perfect in His craft, working flawlessly and providing equal gifts to all. If Phidias, the great sculptor, struggled with material that was difficult to shape, we should not blame him for doing his best. Likewise, we shouldn't fault a musician for the mistakes of a faulty instrument. Instead, we should recognize that a musician deserves even more praise if he can still draw beautiful music from an instrument with broken strings or faulty notes. When the music is flawed, it is the instrument's fault, not the artist's. Those who listen will respect the musician even more for overcoming such difficulties.

Just like that, my noble audience, we must adjust the strings of our inner selves to match the intentions of the musician. Imagine a musician, without his usual instrument, being asked to create beautiful music. He might find a new way to make the sound, using unfamiliar tools, and amaze his listeners even more. There is a story about a cithara player who had Apollo's favor. While playing a melody, one of the strings on his instrument snapped, but a cicada stepped in with its song to fill the missing notes. Thanks to this divine help, the musician continued his performance without fear and won great praise.

I feel the same, noble listeners, as though when I doubt my own strength, the power of the Supreme Being steps in and fills the melody in my place, giving me the ability to honor the king. The purpose of this speech is to glorify royalty and celebrate their achievements. So let us proceed! The musician has begun, and the lyre is ready. May the beauty and sweetness of the music match the message of our song! Since we are here to praise kings and honor their greatness, let us first give thanks to the good God, the supreme King of the universe. After Him, we will honor the rulers who reflect His image and hold the royal scepter.

Even kings welcome songs that descend from the heavens, step by step, knowing that it is Heaven that grants them victory. So let the singer praise the mighty God of the universe, who is eternal and whose power has no end. He is the greatest of all victors, the source of all triumphs, one after another. Let us now finish this speech so we can honor the kings—those who protect peace and keep everyone safe, who hold their ancient power from the Lord above and receive victory from His hand. These rulers hold shining scepters that signal the trials of war, with triumph already in sight. They are not only given the right to rule but also the power to conquer. Even their march into battle strikes fear into their enemies before the fight begins.

PART 4

This discourse ends where it began, with praise for the Supreme Being and the most holy kings who bring us peace. Just as we started by honoring the Almighty, we now end by returning to that same greatness. Just as the sun nurtures seeds and gathers the fruits with its rays, like divine hands collecting gifts for God, so too do we gather within ourselves the beauty of divine wisdom. After breathing in the sweetness of these heavenly gifts, we must now collect the blessings of this sacred harvest, which God will enrich with His nourishing rains. Even if we had ten thousand mouths and ten thousand voices to glorify the pure God, the Father of Souls, we would still fall short of offering Him the praise He deserves. Just like infants who cannot properly honor their father, but are still forgiven for their efforts, we too receive His mercy.

The greatness of God shines in His ability to rise above all creatures. He is the Beginning, the End, the Center, and the Continuation of all praise. In Him, all beings recognize their source—He is all-powerful and limitless. The same is true of our king. As his children, we love to praise him and ask for his forgiveness, knowing that he has already granted it to us. Just as a father is pleased when his children recognize him, even in their weakness, so too does our king rejoice when we acknowledge him. The universal wisdom that gives life to everything and allows us to honor God is itself a gift from God. Since God is good, He holds within Himself all perfection. Being immortal, He possesses endless peace, and His eternal power brings blessings to the world.

In God's divine order, there is no division or change. All beings in Him are filled with wisdom, and the same divine care governs them all. They are guided by the same intelligence, moved by the same kindness, and united by the same love, creating harmony throughout the universe. Therefore, let us bless God and honor the kings who receive their authority from Him. And since we have begun to praise the kings, let us also glorify the reverence they show toward the Supreme. May God teach us how to honor Him properly, and may He help us in this pursuit. Our highest aim must be to revere God and celebrate the kings, for they bring us the peace we enjoy.

The virtue of the king lies in his power to create peace, and his very name carries the meaning of peace. He is called king because he leads with reason and calm authority. He surpasses all other rulers, and even his name becomes a symbol of peace. Just the mention of his name can often drive away enemies. His image acts as a beacon of safety in troubled times. The sight of the king alone brings victory, ensures security, and makes us feel invincible.

Some scholars argue that this text, "Asclepios to King Ammon," might not have been written by one of Hermes' disciples, believing it unworthy of someone taught by such a great master. Dr. Menard notes that despite the criticism of the Greeks in the earlier part of the text, it was likely written in Greek, as suggested by the reference to the Greek word for king, "basileus," and the discussion of its meaning from the Greek verb "bainein," meaning "to advance." The text also mentions Phidias and Eunomios, a musician from Locris, showing Greek influence. The description of the sun as a charioteer, along with the reference to the one who "bears the crowns," reflects Greek customs. In Egypt, the sun was usually depicted as traveling across the Nile on a barge.

Because of these points, Dr. Menard suggests that the negative remarks about the Greeks may have been added later to mislead readers about the text's true origin. He also believes that the kings mentioned in this passage might refer to the Roman emperors Valens and Valentinian. However, I respectfully disagree. Whether or not Asclepios wrote these words, I believe the references to "kings" and "royalties" carry a deeper, mystical meaning. If the intention was simply to flatter a ruler, as Dr. Menard suggests, then why would the writer emphasize that the message contains hidden meanings? Everything said about kingship here fits the symbolic nature of Osiris, the divine ruler whose essence lives within all people.

Osiris reflects the supreme Lord of the Universe and represents the ideal form of humanity. That is why, in the Egyptian Book of the Dead, the soul of the deceased is described as "an Osiris." This symbolizes that the higher part of our nature, the true divine self within us, is like Osiris. It is to this inner king—our higher reason and the divine word of God—that we owe our loyalty, devotion, and eternal service.

. . .

Fragments of The Book of Hermes to His Son Tatios

PART 1

Trismegistus: Out of love for humanity and respect for God, my son, I begin writing this. There is no higher religion than to reflect on the universe and express gratitude to the Creator, and this is something I will always do.

Tatios: Father, if nothing here on Earth is real, how can we use our lives wisely?

Trismegistus: Be religious, my son. Religion is elevated philosophy, and without philosophy, there is no true religion. The person who understands the universe—its laws, principles, and purpose—offers thanks to the Creator, who is like a loving father, a wise teacher, and a faithful protector. This is the essence of religion, for through it, we discover what truth is and where to find it. The more we learn, the deeper our connection to religion becomes. Once the soul, trapped within the body, reaches an understanding of the true Good and Truth, it can never return to ignorance. The power of Love and the forgetting of all evil bind the soul to the Good and prevent it from separating from the Creator.

This is the goal of religion, my son. If you can reach it, your life will be pure, your death will be peaceful, and your soul will know where to go. This is the path that leads to Truth, the same path our ancestors followed to discover the Good. It is a beautiful and steady path, but it is hard for the soul to walk it while trapped in the body. The soul must first struggle with itself, dividing into parts and submitting to its highest aspect. The higher part of the soul fights to rise, while the lower parts—desire and passion—try to drag it down.

If the higher part wins, it builds a defense for itself and its master. But if the lower parts overpower the higher one, the soul is led astray and punished in this life. It is the higher part, my son, that must be your guide. Prepare yourself for the struggle, fight to keep your soul strong, and aim for victory. Now, let me summarize the principles we have discussed. Everything that exists moves, except for things that do not exist. All bodies change, though some only break apart. Not all beings are mortal, nor are all immortal. Things that can break down are corruptible, while those that remain unchanged are eternal.

God comes first, then the universe, and finally humanity. The universe exists for humanity, and humanity exists for God. The emotional part of the soul is mortal, but the rational part is eternal. Every substance is subject to change, yet all true essence is immortal. Everything has two aspects; nothing stays the same forever. Not all things have a soul, but anything that exists is alive through a soul. What is passive can feel, and everything that feels is temporary. All creatures that feel pain and pleasure are mortal, but those that only experience joy without pain are immortal.

Not every body suffers from disease, but anything that can suffer from illness will eventually be destroyed. Intelligence resides in God, and reason in humanity. Reason belongs to intelligence, and intelligence never changes. Nothing physical is fully real, and nothing non-physical is false. Everything that is born undergoes change, though not everything that changes becomes corrupted. There is no perfection on Earth, and no evil in Heaven. God is perfect, while humanity is flawed. Goodness arises through choice, while evil goes against the will. The gods always choose good.

Time belongs to the divine, but law belongs to humanity. Evil feeds the world, while time destroys humans. Everything in Heaven stays the same, while nothing on Earth is unchanging. In Heaven, there is no servitude; on Earth, there is no true freedom. In Heaven, nothing is unknown, while on Earth, nothing is fully understood. There is no connection between celestial things and earthly things. All is perfect in Heaven, and nothing on Earth is free from fault. The immortal knows nothing of death, just as the mortal cannot comprehend immortality. Not everything that is planted will grow, but everything that grows has been planted.

Mortal bodies have two stages of existence: from conception to birth, and from birth to death. Eternal beings, however, exist in a single, unchanging state from the moment they come into being. Mortal bodies increase and decrease. Perishable matter moves between destruction and creation, while immortal essence

112

either remains within itself or transforms into something similar. The birth of one thing brings about the end of another, and every ending is also a beginning.

Some beings exist in physical form, some in pure form, and others in energy. The body contains forms, and forms contain energy. The immortal receives nothing from the mortal, but the mortal can receive from the immortal. Mortal things do not enter immortal forms, but the immortal can dwell in mortal bodies. Energy always moves downward, not upward. What exists on Earth does not benefit what is in Heaven, but everything in Heaven benefits what exists on Earth.

Heaven is filled with immortal beings, while earth holds perishable bodies. The earth is irrational, but heaven is guided by reason. Heavenly things are governed by celestial forces, while earthly things remain on earth. Heaven is the original source of all. Divine providence creates order, and necessity is the tool that providence uses. Chance brings disorder—it is a false image of real energy, only an illusion. God is unchanging Goodness, while man is constantly entangled in evil. If you remember these principles, you will also recall everything I've explained to you in more detail. But be careful about sharing these ideas with the masses. It is not that I want to keep these truths from them, but because exposing them may cause you to become a target for ridicule. Like attracts like, but opposites find no harmony. These teachings should be shared with only a few, or else they might be ignored completely.

There is also a danger in these ideas—if wicked people misuse them, they could become even worse. Stay away from the crowd, for they cannot grasp the value of these teachings.

Tatios: What do you mean, Father?

Trismegistos: Listen closely, my son. Humans are naturally drawn toward evil—it is part of their nature, and they find it pleasing. If people understood that the world was created through divine order and that everything happens because of providence and necessity, they might misuse this knowledge. They could begin to look down on everything that is created, blame destiny for their vices, and indulge in all kinds of wrongdoing. This is why it is wise to avoid sharing these truths with the crowd. Sometimes, ignorance helps keep people within limits, as fear of the unknown can prevent them from acting out.

PART 2

Tatios: You have explained these things clearly, my father, but I still have more questions. You told me that knowledge and skill are activities of reason, and now you say that animals are called "brute" because they lack reason. So does that mean animals cannot possess knowledge or skill?

Trismegistus: Yes, my son, that is correct.

Tatios: But, father, how do you explain animals that seem to display knowledge and skill? For example, ants store food for the winter, birds build nests, and cattle recognize their stables and return to them.

Trismegistus: These actions are not guided by knowledge or skill, my son, but by nature. Knowledge and skill are things we acquire, but these creatures have learned nothing. What they do comes from universal nature. Knowledge and skill belong only to those who acquire them. Actions that are shared by all creatures are natural, not learned. For example, all people can see with their eyes, but not everyone becomes a musician, an archer, or a hunter. Only a few people learn a specific skill or craft and put it to use. If only some ants stored food while others didn't, then you could say those ants possessed the skill of gathering provisions. But since they all behave the same way without deliberate thought, it is clear that neither knowledge nor skill directs them.

Activities, my son, are not physical; they exist within the body and are carried out through the body. Because they are not physical, they are immortal in a sense. But since they must be expressed through a body, they always appear within a body. Anything that has a purpose, determined by divine will and necessity, cannot remain idle. What exists will continue to exist, and that is its life and purpose. This is why bodies will always exist, for the creation of bodies is an eternal function. Even though earthly bodies are corruptible, they are necessary as vessels and tools for the energies that flow through them. Energies are immortal, and because they are immortal, they are always active.

The creation of bodies is ongoing and endless. The abilities of the soul do not all appear at once. Some abilities are present from birth, within the nonrational part of the soul, while the higher abilities emerge as the soul grows in wisdom over time. These abilities are linked to the body, but they come from divine forms and flow into mortal forms, creating bodies. Each ability serves a function, either of the body or the soul, but these abilities remain within the soul even when not connected to a body. The energies are eternal, but the soul is not always confined within a mortal body. The soul can exist without the body, but the abilities cannot manifest unless they have a body to work through.

This is a deep truth, my son. The body cannot exist without the soul, but being itself can.

Tatios: What do you mean by that, father?

Trismegistus: Listen carefully, Tatios. When the soul leaves the body, the body remains, but it begins to break down from within until it completely dissolves. Such a process requires an active force, so even after the soul departs, some energy remains in the body. The difference between an immortal being and a mortal being is this: the immortal being is made of pure, simple essence, while the mortal being is not. One is active and governs, while the other is passive and obeys. One is free, while the other is ruled. Energies are present not only in living beings but also in lifeless things like wood, stone, and similar objects. Through energy, these things grow, ripen, decay, decompose, and change. Energy is what causes transformation, and all becoming is part of the universal process.

There will never be a time when the universe lacks new life, for it constantly produces and destroys beings. Energy itself can never be destroyed, no matter what form it takes or where it manifests. Some energies work through divine beings, others through mortal beings. Some energies are universal, affecting many, while others

116

are specific, working on individual beings. Divine energies operate within eternal beings and are as perfect as those beings themselves.

Partial energies act through living beings, while specific energies operate within everything that exists. This means, my son, that the entire universe is filled with energies. Since energies need bodies to manifest, and there are many bodies in the universe, we can see how abundant these energies are. However, there are even more energies than bodies because one body can hold multiple energies—sometimes one, two, or three—on top of those energies that exist everywhere. I call these universal energies the ones that cannot be separated from bodies, which show themselves through sensations and movements. Without these universal energies, no body could exist.

In contrast, specific energies appear in the minds of humans through art, science, and labor. Sensations come with energies or result from them. Understand, my son, the difference between energy and sensation. Energy comes from a higher place, while sensation belongs to the body and depends on it. The body serves as a seat or vehicle for energy, allowing the energy to express itself through it. For this reason, I say that sensations are tied to the body and are mortal. Their existence begins and ends with the body. On the other hand, immortal energies do not have sensations because of their nature. Sensations can only arise from some good or bad experience affecting the body, and immortal beings are not subject to these changes.

Tatios: So, does every body experience sensation?

Trismegistus: Yes, my son, every body experiences sensation, and energies act in all bodies.

Tatios: Even in lifeless things, father?

Trismegistus: Yes, even in lifeless things. Sensations vary by type. In beings with reason, sensations are accompanied by thought. In beings without reason, sensations are purely physical. In lifeless things, sensations take the form of passive processes, such as growth and decay. Both passion and sensation are the result of energies, coming from a single source and leading to a single outcome.

In living beings, two more energies accompany passion and sensation: joy and sorrow. Without these, no living being—and especially no reasonable being—would be able to feel anything. Therefore, joy and sorrow can be seen as forms of emotion in all living beings. They appear through sensations, as movements within the body, driven by the irrational parts of the soul. Both joy and sorrow are forms of suffering. Joy, which is the feeling of pleasure, often brings about greater troubles. Sorrow leads to pain and punishment, making it equally harmful.

Tatios: Is sensation the same thing in both the soul and the body, father?

Trismegistus: What do you mean by the sensation of the soul, my son?

Tatios: The soul is not physical, father. But sensation seems to be tied to the body, since it exists within it.

Trismegistus: If we say that sensation belongs to the body, then we must compare it either to the soul or to the energies, which are not physical, even though they exist within the body. However, sensation is neither an energy nor a soul, nor is it separate from the body. Therefore, it cannot be something non-physical. If it isn't non-physical, it must be physical, because nothing exists that is neither physical nor non-physical.

PART 3

The Lord, the Creator of immortal forms, Tatios, completed His work and made nothing more. He does not create anything new now either. Once these eternal forms were given life and connected to one another, they began to move on their own, needing nothing to sustain them. Even if they rely on each other in some ways, they do not need anything outside themselves because they are immortal. This is how the creations of the supreme God are meant to be.

However, our immediate creator, the one who made us, has a body. He created us and continues to create mortal bodies that are subject to change and decay. Unlike the supreme Creator, he cannot create immortal beings, nor should he try to imitate Him. The supreme God created eternal forms from His own essence, which is incorporeal. But our creator formed us from material substances, giving us physical bodies that are naturally weak and dependent on external support.

Because we are made of physical matter, we need constant nourishment and renewal to survive. The earth, water, fire, and air flow into us, restoring and sustaining our bodies. Without these elements replenishing us, the combination of substances that make up our bodies would fall apart. We are so fragile that we cannot even remain active for a full day without rest. You know well, my son, that without the night's rest, our bodies could not endure the strain of the day's work.

In His wisdom, our good creator has provided for our survival by creating sleep, which restores movement and strength. He made sure that the time spent resting is equal to or even longer than the time spent working. Think, my son, about how sleep serves the body and how important it is, even though it contrasts with the soul's constant activity. If the soul's function is to keep moving, the body relies on sleep to loosen the tension within and restore what it needs. Sleep provides the body with water to nourish the blood, earth for the bones, air for the nerves and vessels, and fire for the eyes. This is why the body finds such pleasure in sleep.

The teachings of Hermetic philosophy reflect the idea that divine energy flows constantly into the universe, even though the forms through which it flows remain unchanged and self-sustaining. The natural order was set from the beginning and cannot be altered. The soul's journey into physical life is an ongoing process and will only end when the creative cycle is complete. The flow of divine energy has never stopped since the beginning of creation. Life continues to emerge because of this constant outpouring of being into existence, and without it, the process of creation and evolution would halt. The creator mentioned here is the Demiurge, the one responsible for shaping the physical universe.

PART 4

A great and divine power, my son, is placed at the center of the universe, observing everything that people do on earth. In the divine order, everything is guided by providential Necessity, while among people, this role is fulfilled by Justice. The first order governs heavenly things, for the Gods neither wish to, nor are able to, break any laws. They cannot make mistakes, and because mistakes lead to sin, they are free from sin.

The second order, Justice, is responsible for correcting the wrongs that happen among people on earth. Since humans are mortal and made of corruptible matter, they are prone to losing their way when they no longer focus on divine things to guide them toward virtue. This is where Justice steps in to act.

Through the energies he draws from Nature, man is subject to Destiny. But through the mistakes he makes in life, man is subject to Justice.

PART 5

Here, then, is what can be said about the three aspects of time. They do not exist independently, and they are not completely separate from each other. Yet, in another way, they are both connected and distinct. Can we imagine the present without the past? One cannot exist without the other, because the present is created by the past, and the future emerges from the present.

If we want to fully understand this, we need to reason like this: The past has already moved into what no longer exists. The future does not exist until it becomes the present. And the present, in turn, stops being itself the moment it passes. How can we call something present when it doesn't stay for even an instant and has no fixed point? If it vanishes as soon as it appears, can it really be said to exist?

Moreover, since the past is closely tied to the present, and the present connects directly to the future, they blend into one. They share an identity, unity, and continuity. Time flows without interruption, constantly moving and changing, even though it remains one and the same.

PART 6

My son, matter is always in the process of becoming. It has existed before, and it continues to change, for matter serves as the vehicle for transformation. Becoming is how the uncreated and all-knowing God expresses His activity. Matter carries within it the seed of change, and through this seed, it is brought into existence. The creative force shapes matter according to ideal forms, giving it structure. Before it is formed, matter has no shape or identity. It only takes on form when it is put into motion through creation.

PART 7

It is impossible for a human, who is imperfect and made up of many flawed parts, to speak with certainty about what is truly real, my son Tatios. Our bodies are formed from different elements that are not originally part of us. Still, as much as I can, I say that reality only exists in eternal beings, for their forms are truly real.

Fire is simply fire, earth is only earth, and air is only air. But our bodies are made of a combination of these elements—fire, earth, water, and air—yet our bodies are not really fire, earth, water, or air, nor anything truly real.

Since reality has never been a part of us from the start, how could we ever see it, speak of it, or even understand it unless God allows us to? The things of this world are not truly real but only copies of reality. In fact, not all things are even proper copies; some are nothing more than illusions and errors, mere tricks of the mind. When something receives a spark of higher truth, it can become a reflection of the real. Without this divine influence, it stays an illusion. It is like a portrait: a painting of a person, but not the person it represents. It may have eyes, but it cannot see; it may have ears, but it cannot hear. A portrait only gives the appearance of a person but is nothing more than an image that fools the eye. It seems real but is only a shadow. Those who avoid being deceived by false appearances see what is true. If we can see things as they are, we understand the real, but if we only see what is false, we cannot understand or know the real at all.

Tatios: So, is there anything truly real on earth, my father?

Trismegistus: Reality does not exist on earth, my son, and it cannot be found here. However, a few people may grasp it if God grants them the gift of divine vision. What exists on earth is only made up of appearances and opinions, not reality itself. And yet, reality can be found through intelligence and reason. To think and speak the truth is as close as we come to what is real.

Tatios: But how can that be? How can we think and speak truthfully if nothing on earth is real?

Trismegistus: It is true, my son, that we know nothing of absolute Truth. How could it be otherwise? Truth is the highest virtue, the ultimate Good. It is not clouded by matter or trapped in physical form. It is pure, unchanging, and eternal. But the things here on earth, as you see, are not compatible with the Good. They are temporary, always changing, and constantly shifting from one form to another. How can something be real if it cannot even remain the same as itself? Anything that is always changing is not just an illusion in itself, but it also deceives us by appearing in different ways at different times.

Tatios: Does this mean that even man is not real, father?

Trismegistus: No, my son. Man is not real in the truest sense. Reality only belongs to something that remains the same and stays true to itself. Man, on the other hand, is made up of many different parts and never stays the same. As long as he lives in a body, he changes from one age to another, from one state to the next. Sometimes, after only a short while, parents no longer recognize their children, and children no longer recognize their parents. Can something that changes so much that it is no longer recognizable be considered real? Should we not see these ever-changing forms as illusions? Only what is eternal and good can be considered real. Man is temporary, and therefore not real; he is just an appearance, and appearances are the ultimate illusion.

Tatios: So even the stars and celestial bodies are not real, since they also change?

Trismegistus: Anything that is born and subject to change cannot be real. However, the works of the great Creator can receive a kind of reality from Him. Still, even they contain an element of falsehood because they change, and nothing can be truly real unless it remains the same.

Tatios: Then what can we call truly real, my father?

Trismegistus: The sun is the only being among all creatures that does not change and remains constant. This is why it is given the task of overseeing the universe. It is the leader and creator of all things. I honor the sun and bow before its truth. After the One, it is the second creator I recognize.

Tatios: What, then, is the original Reality, father?

Trismegistus: He is the One and only, Tatios, who is not made of matter, who does not exist within any body. He has no color, no shape, and He never changes. He simply *is*. Anything that is an illusion will perish, my son. The order of the Real ensures that everything in this world will end through dissolution, for the cycle of birth depends on things breaking apart. Everything that is created must eventually dissolve, only to be born again. From dissolution, life emerges, and life must also decay, so that creation can continue without end.

See, then, the Creator who existed before everything. The things born from dissolution are just shadows; they shift and change, becoming one thing today and another tomorrow. They can never remain the same, and how can something that is always changing be truly real? Such things are mere appearances, my son. Man, too, is only an appearance of Humanity, just as a child represents childhood, a youth represents adolescence, a grown man represents adulthood, and an old man represents old age. How can we say that a child remains a child, or a man remains the same man, when constant changes hide what they were and what they have become?

So understand, my son, that all these things are only illusions reflecting a higher Reality. Since this is the case, I define illusion as a reflection of what is truly Real.

It is difficult to understand God, and it is impossible to describe Him. The physical world cannot express the non-physical, and something imperfect cannot fully grasp what is perfect. How can the eternal be connected with the temporary? The eternal remains forever, while the temporary quickly passes away. What is eternal is Real, while what is temporary is only a faint reflection. The difference between the mortal and the divine is as great as the difference between weakness and strength, or smallness and greatness. This distance between them clouds our understanding of true beauty.

We can see physical things with our eyes, and what the eyes perceive, the tongue can describe. But what has no body, no appearance, no shape, and no form cannot be understood by the senses. I know, Tatios, that God cannot be fully described. He is beyond anything we can define or explain.

● ● ●

126

Fragments of The Writings of Hermes to Ammon

PART 1

The force that governs the universe is Providence. What holds the universe together and sets its boundaries is Necessity. Destiny drives and controls everything with the power it possesses. It is Destiny that causes both the beginning of life and its end. Providence comes first and gives order to the universe. It reaches to the heavens, where the gods move in endless, tireless motion. Destiny exists because Necessity exists. Providence sees what is to come, and Destiny decides the arrangement of the stars. This is the universal law.

PART 2

Everything is brought into existence by Nature and Destiny, and no place is beyond the reach of Providence. Providence is the free will of the Supreme God, from which two natural forces arise: Necessity and Destiny. Destiny follows the guidance of both Providence and Necessity, while the stars follow the path set by

Destiny. No one can escape from Destiny or defend themselves against the influence of the stars, as they act as tools of Destiny. Through them, the will of Destiny is carried out across all of Nature and in the lives of human beings.

PART 3

The soul is an essence that has no physical form, and even when it is within a body, it does not lose its true nature. Its essence lies in constant movement—the free movement of thought. Yet the soul does not move through anything, towards anything, or for any specific purpose. It is a primal force, and what is primary does not rely on anything secondary.

The phrase "in anything" refers to place, time, and nature. "Towards anything" refers to harmony, shape, or structure. "For anything" refers to the body, since time, place, nature, and form are connected to the body. All these elements are tied together in a cycle of mutual dependence. A body requires a place, because it cannot exist without occupying space. A body changes its nature, and such change must happen over time, through movement in nature. The parts of a body cannot come together without harmony in form.

Space exists because of physical bodies. It holds their changes and prevents them from being lost as they transform. A body shifts from one state to another, but even when it leaves one state, it remains a body; it just takes on a new condition. It is still a body—only its state has changed. This means that what shifts in a body is not its essence, but its qualities and way of being.

Place, time, and natural movement are not physical things, but each has its own unique role. The role of space is to contain. The role of time is to mark intervals and measure change. The role of nature is movement. The role of harmony is connection. The role of the body is to change. And the role of the soul is to think.

PART 4

The soul is an essence without a physical form. If it had a body, it could not preserve itself, because every body needs breath and life, which depend on order. Wherever something is born, it is always changing. To "become" implies growth, and growth brings increase, but every increase eventually leads to decrease, which brings about destruction. Anything that receives the form of life can only exist through the soul. For something to exist, it must already be part of life. I define existence as the process of becoming reasonable and participating in intelligent life. Life creates the creature, intelligence makes it reasonable, and the body makes it mortal.

The soul has no physical form and holds an unchanging power. Can a being be intelligent without a living soul? Can it be rational if there is no intelligent force guiding its rational life? Intelligence does not show itself equally in all creatures because the way their bodies are formed affects their harmony. If a body contains too much heat, the creature becomes restless and energetic. If cold dominates, the creature becomes sluggish and heavy. Nature arranges the elements of the body according to a balance or harmony. This balance comes in three forms: hot, cold, and balanced or temperate.

The way these elements combine in a body depends on the influence of the stars. The soul takes the body that is destined for it and gives it life through the work of nature. Nature matches the harmony within the body to the arrangement of the stars, aligning the elements in the body with the harmony of the heavens. This creates a mutual connection, where the stars and the body reflect each other. The purpose of this stellar harmony is to create sympathies that align with destiny.

PART 5

The soul, Ammon, is an essence that exists for its own purpose, receiving the life it was given from the start. It draws to itself a certain kind of reason mixed with passion and desire. Passion is like a raw material; when it aligns with the intelligent part of the soul, it becomes courage, standing firm against fear. Desire, too, is a raw material; when it works alongside the rational part of the soul, it turns into aspiration and resists indulgence. Reason acts like a light, guiding and correcting the blindness of desire. When the soul's different abilities are balanced under the control of reason, they create justice.

The management of the soul's abilities belongs to the Intellectual Principle, which functions with its own thoughtful reason. It governs everything like a judge, with its reason acting as its advisor. This Principle understands how reason can guide even the irrational parts, giving them a form of rationality. Though this rationality is weaker than true reason, it still surpasses the irrational—much like how an echo reflects a voice or how the moon reflects the sun's light. Passion and desire follow their own patterns of reason, attracting each other and creating a flow of thought between them.

Every soul is immortal and always in motion. Movement either comes from energy or from the body. Since the soul is without a physical form, it does not come from matter but from an essence that is also non-material. Everything that is born must come from something else. All things that are born and eventually decay involve two kinds of movement: the soul moves the being to life, while the body grows, shrinks, and decomposes as it breaks down. This is the cycle of perishable bodies. But the soul itself is in constant motion, never stopping. It moves by its own nature, creating movement from within. Every soul, therefore, is immortal because it is always in motion.

There are three kinds of souls: divine, human, and irrational. The divine soul exists in a divine form, which gives it the energy to move and act. When this soul leaves mortal beings, it abandons its irrational parts and returns to its divine form. Because the divine soul is always in motion, it flows along with the universal movement. The human soul also contains something divine, but it is bound to irrational elements like desire and passion. These irrational parts are energies, and although they are tied to mortal bodies, they do not die. However, they are separate from the divine part of the soul, which belongs to the divine form. When the divine part enters a mortal body and meets these irrational elements, it becomes a human soul.

The soul of animals is made up of passion and desire, which is why animals are called brutes—they lack reason. The fourth type of soul is the one connected to lifeless things. This soul exists outside the bodies it influences. It moves within the divine form and passively directs the objects it touches.

PART 6

The soul is an eternal and intelligent essence, guided by its own reason. It aligns itself with the concept of harmony. Even when it is separated from the physical body, the soul continues to exist on its own, independent in the world of ideals. It governs its reason and gives life a movement similar to its own thought—this is the essence of being, for the soul's nature is to shape other things according to its own character.

There are two types of life movements: one that matches the essence of the soul, and one that follows the nature of the body. The first type is universal and free, while the second is specific and bound by necessity. Everything that moves must follow the laws of whatever causes its movement. However, the soul's movement is connected by its nature to the principle of intelligence. The soul must be without a physical form and entirely distinct from the body because, if it had a body, it could not have reason or thought. All bodies lack intelligence, but when they receive the spirit, they become alive and breathe.

Breath belongs to the body, while reason focuses on the beauty of what is essential. The spirit connected to the senses interprets appearances. This spirit is divided among the different senses, such as sight, hearing, smell, taste, and touch. It interacts with thought to make sense of sensations; without thought, it only produces illusions because it belongs to the body and passively

132

receives everything. Judgment belongs to reason, which understands higher things, while opinion belongs to the sensory spirit. The sensory spirit draws its energy from the outside world, while reason finds its energy within itself.

• • •

Various Hermetic Fragments

PART 1

There are essential spirit, reason, intelligence, and perception. Opinion and sensation lean toward perception, while reason aligns with the essential spirit. Thought moves independently but is also connected to perception. When combined, these elements form the soul. Opinion and sensation aim for perfection but do not stay consistent. They can shift between excess, deficiency, or change. Without perception, they decline, but when they follow perception closely, they connect with intellectual reason through learning and knowledge.

We have the power to choose, and it is up to us whether we select the best or the worst path by our will. Choosing what is harmful ties us to the physical world and places us under the control of Destiny. However, the intellectual spirit within us is free, and because of that, our reason is also free, unchanging, and beyond the reach of Destiny. When we follow this higher, intelligent reason, which is guided by the will of the supreme God, the spirit rises above the natural order of created things. But when the soul becomes attached to these created things, it becomes connected to their destiny, even though it is not truly part of their nature.

PART 2

There is a state of Being that is higher than all other beings and everything that exists. This Being is what gives universal essence to everything that is real and intelligible. Nature is the essence we can sense, containing within itself all physical objects. Between these two realms are the intellectual gods and the gods of the senses. The thoughts of intelligence connect with the intellectual gods, while opinions align with the gods of the senses, who reflect the higher intelligences. For example, the sun is a reflection of the creative and celestial God. Just as God created the universe, the sun brings animals to life, causes plants to grow, and controls the movement of water and other fluids.

PART 3

Thus, the soul's formless vision rises beyond the body to gaze upon true beauty. It lifts itself up in reverence, not for shape, body, or appearance, but for what lies beyond them all—something serene, still, essential, and unchanging. It is everything, complete in itself, singular and whole, existing by and through itself, always the same, without change or variation.

PART 4

If you understand this one and only Good, nothing will be beyond your reach, for all virtue is contained within it. Do not think this Good exists inside anyone or outside of anyone—it has no boundaries, yet it is the boundary of all things. Nothing holds it, but it holds everything within itself. What difference is there between the physical and the non-physical, the created and the uncreated, the things bound by necessity and those that are free, or between earthly things and heavenly things, between what can decay and what is eternal? The difference lies in this: some things exist freely, while others are bound by necessity. What belongs to the lower realm is incomplete and will pass away.

PART 5

Beneath nature and the ideal world stands the pyramid. At its peak is the cornerstone, the Creative Word of the universal Lord. This Word is the first power after Him—uncreated, infinite, and existing before everything He made. It is the child of the Most Perfect, the true and fruitful Son. The nature of this intelligent Word is to generate and create. You may call it generation, nature, or character, but know this: it is perfect in the Perfect, it comes from the Perfect, and all its works are perfectly good. It is the source of both creation and life.

Because this is its nature, it is rightly named. If not for the care and guidance of the universal Lord, who has caused me to share these truths, you would not have such a strong desire to explore these matters. Now, listen to the conclusion of this message. The Spirit I have spoken of so often is essential to all things. It sustains everything, gives life to all beings, and nourishes them. Flowing endlessly from the holy Source, it continually provides support to spirits and all living creatures.

PART 6

The Ideal Light existed before any other light, and the pure Intelligence of Intelligence has always been. Its unity is nothing other than the Spirit that surrounds the entire universe. From this Spirit comes neither gods, nor angels, nor anything else essential, for He is the Lord of all things, the source of power and light. Everything depends on Him and exists within Him. His perfect Word, both generative and creative, descended into the forces of nature and into the waters that bring forth life, making them fruitful.

After saying this, he stood and declared: "I call upon you, Heaven, sacred work of the great God. I call upon you, Voice of the Father, spoken at the beginning when the universe was created. I call upon you, Word, the only Son of the Father, who holds all things together. Be kind, be kind!"

PART 7

Seven planets move along the paths of Olympus, and through them, Eternity is measured: the Moon that lights the night, the dark Kronos, the gentle Sun, the Paphian Goddess who protects marriage, the bold Ares, the fertile Hermes, and Zeus, the source of life and nature's foundation. These planets have also been connected to humanity, for within each of us are the Moon, Zeus, Ares, Aphrodite, Kronos, Phoebus, and Hermes.

From the heavenly essence, we draw our tears, laughter, anger, speech, creation, sleep, and desire. Tears come from Kronos, creation from Zeus, speech from Hermes, courage from Ares, sleep from Artemis, desire from Kytheraea (Aphrodite), and laughter from Apollo, who brings joy to human thoughts and fills the endless world with delight.

PART 8

Hermes teaches that those who know God are protected from the attacks of evil and are no longer bound by Destiny. Knowing God is what true religion means.

• • •

The End

Thank you for Reading

You've Just Read a Piece of the Greatest Library Ever Rebuilt

Thank you for reading.

This book is one of thousands we're restoring, reimagining, and translating as part of the **Modern Library of Alexandria** — a global movement to preserve and share humanity's most important ideas.

What was once lost to fire and time is now rising again — not just as memory, but as living, breathing knowledge, freely accessible to all.

What You Can Do Next:

- **Keep Reading.**

  Discover more legendary works — in beautiful print, audiobook, or digital form — at LibraryofAlexandria.com.

- **Build Your Own Library.**

  Every title is available as a paperback, hardcover, or collectible boxset — at true printing cost. Craft a personal library worthy of display.

- **Spread the Light.**

  Share this book. Tell others about the movement. Help us translate every timeless work into every language, so no reader is ever left behind.

By finishing this book, you've already taken part in something extraordinary.

Join us at LibraryofAlexandria.com

Together, we're rebuilding the greatest library the world has ever known.

With appreciation,
The Modern Library of Alexandria Team

Visit:

www.libraryofalexandria.com

Or scan the code below: